A Theory of the Mechanism of Survival

Mechanism of Survival

The Fourth Dimension and Its Applications

W. Whately Smith

Alpha Editions

This edition published in 2023

ISBN : 9789357941242

Design and Setting By
Alpha Editions
www.alphaedis.com
Email - info@alphaedis.com

Contents

PREFACE

The highly speculative and extrapolatory character of this book will be evident to all who are bold enough to read it.

I wish to make it perfectly clear that I have no intention of dogmatising on so obscure a subject. The suggestions which follow are purely tentative, and I am well aware that some of them are likely to prove mutually incompatible.

But it is only by the bold formulation and ruthless rejection of hypotheses that progress is made, and even if we are compelled to abandon the Higher Space Hypothesis altogether—as is very possible—the negative information so gained will be of the greater value if the hypothesis has first been given the fullest possible trial.

W.W.S.

CHAPTER I

THE MEANING OF FOUR-DIMENSIONAL SPACE.

The main line of thought developed in these pages has no claims to originality. Professor Zöllner of Leipsic was an ardent exponent of the theory in the "seventies" and some authors hold that even the ancient writings of the East contain attempts to express Four-Dimensional concepts.

Whether this is actually so is open to doubt but it must be remembered that in the days when these writings were produced mathematical knowledge was itself in its infancy and that there was, therefore, no terminology available in which the Higher Space concepts could be suitably expressed even supposing that the ancient philosophers had them in mind.

It is only through accumulated knowledge, especially the work of Gauss, Lobatschewsky, Bolyai, Riemann, and others that modern mathematicians are able to deal easily with space of more than three dimensions.

It may be noted that Kant says:

"If it be possible that there are developments of other dimensions of space, it is very probable that God has somewhere produced them. For His works have all the grandeur and glory that can be comprised."

According to Mr. G.R.S. Mead similar ideas are to be found in certain of the Gnostic cosmogonies.

(Fragments of a Faith forgotten, p. 318.)

But a detailed historical review would be out of place here and I will therefore proceed at once to a discussion of what is meant by the term "fourth dimension" and will try to explain how it is that we can determine some of the necessary properties of four-dimensional space, even although we cannot picture it to ourselves.

At this point I would urge the reader to try to believe that the subject is not one of great difficulty. As a matter of fact it is really exceptionally straightforward if only one faces it and does not allow oneself to be frightened.

I know that it is impossible to form any clear mental picture of four-dimensional conditions, but that does not matter. The ideas involved are admittedly unprecedented in our experience, but they are not contrary to reason and I do not ask more than a formal and intellectual assent to the propositions and analogies concerned.

Let me start, then, by defining what is meant by a Dimension. The best definition I can think of is to say that, in the sense in which the word is used here, a Dimension means "An independent direction in space."

I must amplify this by saying that, "Two directions in space are to be considered as independent when they are so related that no movement, however great, along one of them will result in the slightest movement along, or parallel to, the other. That is to say, at right angles, or perpendicular to one another."

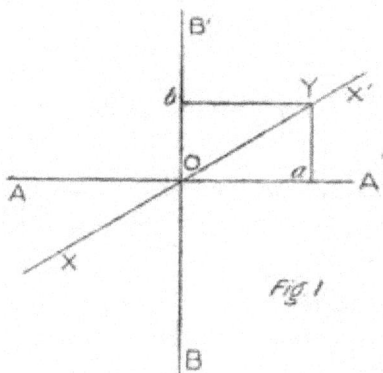

Fig. 1

Thus in Fig. 1 AOA´ and BOB´ are independent directions. One might move for ever along OA or OA´ and yet one would not have moved in the very least in the direction of OB or of OB´.

Now on a flat surface, such as a sheet of paper, it is not possible to draw more than *two* such directions. Any other line that can be drawn, XOX´ for instance, is in a compound direction, so to speak. That is to say it is partly in the direction AOA´ and partly in the direction BOB´ and it is possible to reach any point in it, Y for example, by moving along OA´ to *a* and then moving in the direction of OB´ a distance equal to O*b*, or *vice versa* or by doing the two simultaneously.

For the benefit of those who are absolutely ignorant of the rudiments of Geometrical knowledge, I would point out that Parallel lines are said to point, in fact *do* point, in the same direction.

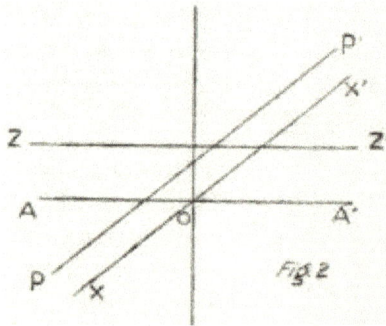

Fig. 2

Thus, in Fig. 2, the direction of the line ZZ´ is the same as that of AOA´ and the direction of the line PP´ is the same as that of XOX´.

Thus we see that in a flat surface we find only *two* dimensions and consequently we can refer to a flat surface as "Space of two dimensions" or "Two-dimensional space."

But if we refuse to be restricted to a flat surface we find that it is possible to draw a third line through O which is quite "independent" of the directions of the two lines we have previously drawn. We can do this by drawing it vertically, that is to say, perpendicular to the plane of the paper. Call this line COC´.

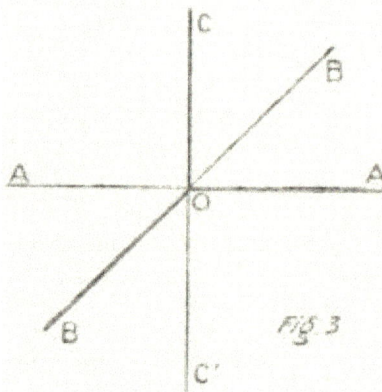

Fig. 3

I have shown it *in perspective* in Fig. 3. This line fulfils the definition we gave of an independent direction in space for it is at right angles both to AOA´ and to BOB´. But we have now exhausted our resources. Try as we will we are unable to draw a fourth line which shall be at right angles to AOA´, BOB´, and COC´ simultaneously.

On other words—In the space we know we find only three dimensions and consequently we can refer to it as "Space of three dimensions" or "Three-dimensional space."

Now the idea of a fourth dimension of space is simply this: That, whereas in three-dimensional space, we can draw, through any point in it, *three*, and only three, lines mutually at right angles: in four-dimensional space, it would be possible to draw, through any point in it, *four*, and only four, lines mutually at right angles.

Extending the idea to "Higher space" in general, we may say that,—In space of "n" dimensions we can draw, through any point in it, "n," and only "n," lines mutually at right angles.

Now I admit, that, at first sight, the idea that it might be possible, under any circumstances, to draw more than three such lines through a point, seems utterly staggering and inconceivable. And indeed the more one thinks of it and the more thoroughly one grasps what it means, the more absolutely impossible does it appear.

All the same, as I hope to show very soon, it *is*, as a matter of fact, quite possible that there may be another independent direction fulfilling the prescribed conditions, in spite of the fact that we are at present ignorant of it.

This we can only realize by a consideration of the time-honoured but indispensable analogy of a two-dimensional world, or "Flatland."

This analogy I propose to examine in some detail in the paragraphs which follow.

But before doing so I wish to point out, and I do not think it will be necessary to do more, that a "line" which has length, but neither breadth nor thickness, can be correctly described as "One-dimensional space" *i.e.*:—space having only one dimension.

A mathematical "point," which has only position and neither length nor breadth nor thickness, can similarly be called space of no dimensions or "Zero-dimensional space." Also I wish to take the opportunity of defining one or two words which I may have occasion to use and have the merit of brevity.

(1) Lines which are drawn through a point for the sake of determining direction are called in Geometrical parlance, "Axes."

Thus in Fig. 1 AOA′ and BOB′ are axes. The former would be known as "the axis of A," the latter as "the axis of B." Similarly in Fig. 3 COC′ is "the axis of C."

(2) The point in which two or more axes meet, is called the "Origin" and is commonly denoted by the letter O.

(3) When convenient, I shall use the terms, "Two space," "Three space," "Four space," etc., instead of writing "Two-dimensional space," "Three-dimensional space," "Four-dimensional space," etc. in full each time.

THE ANALOGY OF A TWO-DIMENSIONAL WORLD.

The consideration of the analogy of a two dimensional world is necessary because, as Mr. C.H. Hinton says in his book, "The Fourth Dimension," p. 6.

"The change in our conceptions, which we make in passing from the shapes and motions in two dimensions to those in three, affords a pattern by which we can pass on still further to the conception of an existence in four-dimensional space."

Let us start then by imagining a very large, flat and perfectly smooth surface; such for instance as the top of a highly polished table or the surface of a sheet of still liquid.

We have seen that such a surface constitutes space of two dimensions, because through any point in it we can only draw two lines at right angles to one another. In order to draw a third such line we must get out of the surface altogether and draw the line perpendicular to it.

Next we must try to imagine that this surface is populated by a race of beings of an extraordinary thinness.

In order to grasp the analogy properly we must imagine them to be so constituted that they are incapable of realising any direction in space which does not lie in the aforementioned flat surface on which they live.

We can imagine this by supposing that their thickness, *i.e.*:—their extension in the third dimension perpendicular to their surface,—is so small as to be invisible to them and also that their "nerve endings" all lie on their periphery. This last is equivalent to saying that they have no "sense organs" facing the third dimension and that therefore they cannot receive impressions, or respond to any stimuli that come to them from that direction.

It follows, therefore, that unless they develope special sense organs which face the third dimension they will be acquainted only with such objects and events as lie, or take place, in their surface.

It is of course inconceivable that they should be truly "plane" beings in the mathematical sense and possess no thickness at all. But if we suppose that their thickness is of the same order as the diameter of a chemical "Atom"—that they are "one atom thick" so to speak,—the conditions laid down as to their limitation will be fulfilled.

Now we have supposed the flat surface in our analogy to be *perfectly* smooth in the true sense of the word. That is to say of such a nature as to offer no resistance whatever to the passage of objects over it.

This means that plane beings will not be sensible of any opposition to their movement as far as the surface is concerned. Also, as we have supposed that they have no nerve endings facing it, it follows that they cannot feel any pressure from it. In short they will be totally unaware of its existence.

But for the purpose of strict analogy this is insufficient, because a being placed on such a surface would be as incapable of movement as we should be if we were freely suspended in infinite space, remote from all the material objects we know. There would be nothing, in any direction known to him, from which he could "push off." We must therefore further suppose that the force of gravity operates in his world in a manner similar to that which we know,—every particle of matter attracting every other particle.

This will mean two things; first, that every particle on the surface will be held against that surface and that plane beings will, therefore, never be able to move away from it; and, second, that matter on the surface will tend to collect together in a manner precisely analogous to what we observe in our space.

Finally, we may suppose that these hypothetical beings whom we are considering live on the rim of a very large disc of plane matter, which has collected and is held together by the action of gravity, just as we live on the surface of a very large sphere of solid matter. They will be kept up against the rim of the disc by the force of gravity, which will attract them towards its centre, in the same way that we are kept against the surface of the earth.

It is easy to realise that the existence of such a plane being will be very limited indeed. He will be conscious of two directions only. One will be "up and down" that is to say, towards or away from the centre of his plane earth: the other will be "forwards and backwards" along its rim. Again any object, that projects beyond the rim of the disc on which he lives, will be for him an obstacle, which can only be passed by climbing over or burrowing under it. He cannot go round it, because that would mean coming out of the flat surface, which he is unable to do. Thus in Fig. 4, if the curved line AB represents a portion of the rim of the disc or "plane earth," and C a plane being, then he can only pass from A to B by "climbing over" any intervening object such as D, *i.e.*:—by following the path indicated by the dotted line.

Otherwise he would have to get out of the plane of the paper, which is impossible for him.

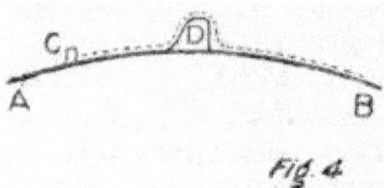

Fig. 4

Now that I have described in outline the strict analogy of a race of plane beings inhabiting a smooth surface, I shall take the liberty, in the course of developing the idea more fully, of treating it in a slightly less rigid fashion. That is to say I shall assume that the reader has grasped the main idea and I shall not trouble about the "Plane earth" etc., unless it is desirable to do so for the sake of bringing out some special point; and I shall substitute for the foregoing somewhat elaborate representation the simpler one of a thin object free to slide on a smooth surface lying in front of us.

But before doing so I would point out that already we begin to see our way a little. We can understand for instance that the fact of a Fourth dimension of space being unknown and inconceivable to us, is no proof that it does not exist. We have seen that a Third dimension would be equally unknown and inconceivable to a being limited in the manner described above; although we know that a third dimension does exist.

We have only to suppose that analogous limitations obtain in our own case to see that a Fourth dimension might well exist of which we would still be unaware.

We must, for instance, suppose that we have no sense organs facing that way and that we are prevented from moving in that direction by some circumstance analogous to the smooth sheet on which we supposed the plane being to live. The plane being would think that he could see all round his plane objects although we know that he could not really do so, and similarly our conviction that we can see all round our solid objects may be an illusion.

Thus we are already in a position to appreciate the fact that our inability to perceive or imagine Four-dimensional space or objects in it, is no argument against its existence. There is, therefore, no 'a priori' reason for supposing that four dimensional space is not a reality. It is a point which must be settled by an appeal to the evidence.

If, in the course of our investigation, we find that there are in our space phenomena, which closely resemble those which would in "two space" indicate the existence of a third dimension, then we shall be entitled to say that these phenomena indicate the probable existence of a fourth dimension.

We can now proceed with our consideration of a two dimensional world, remembering that,—

Shapes and events in four space bear to shapes and events in three space, the same relation that those in three space bear to those in two space.

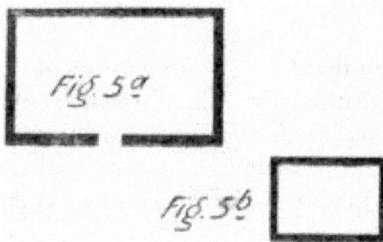

Fig. 5[a]
Fig. 5[b]

The very small three-dimensional thickness which we have supposed to exist in all the objects of our plane world is imperceptible to the plane beings which inhabit it and the objects which they perceive they will accordingly think of as geometrical figures and of their boundaries as geometrical lines, having length but no breadth. A circle will appear to a plane being as a completely closed space. He will, as he thinks, be able to go all round it without being able to find any opening in its bounding line. It will in fact be to him what a sphere is to us. A two space room will be a thing like the figure shown in Fig. 5a. He will be able to get into or out of it by the gap in the wall which is shown and which corresponds to the door. But he will not be able to conceive of any other mode of entry or exit, although we can see that from the direction of the third dimension it is not closed at all. Similarly, if Fig. 5b represents a closed two-dimensional box, we see that this is absolutely open to us, who are three dimensional beings, though appearing to be closed on all sides to a plane being. If we took advantage of this fact we could play all sorts of tricks on him for we could put things into the box or take them out of it, by way of the third dimension, while to the plane being the box would appear to be tightly closed the whole time. It will be noticed that as the path of an object in transference would lie wholly outside the plane being's space he would not be able to form any conception of the nature of the process involved. If he tried to understand it at all he would probably imagine that the object has been disintegrated into particles inside the box, passed in this condition through the minute interstices which he might suppose to exist in its walls, and reintegrated on the other side. Whereas the true explanation is far simpler. The very great importance of this will become apparent when we come to consider the question of the positive evidences for the existence of a fourth dimension.

It is because of this importance that I have dwelt on a point which to many readers will have been obvious as soon as stated.

Similarly we could make things appear "from nowhere" and disappear equally mysteriously simply by putting them down on to his flat surface and picking them up again.

I may as well repeat here that I do not for a moment expect that the reader will have been able to visualise four-dimensional space. But I do hope that he will have seen the force of the analogy and will be prepared to admit that so far as we have gone at present four dimensional space is by no means inconceivable though it may not be distinctly imaginable.

The foregoing is really all that is necessary on the mathematical or theoretical side for the understanding of the basic ideas with which I am dealing but for the benefit of those readers who like that sort of thing I have added a few simple propositions and extensions of the analogy in the form of an appendix.

The only other question that need really concern us here is that of the phenomena of *change* in a two-dimensional world.

We have already seen that a cube laid on a flat surface will present to a plane being, in that surface, the appearance of a square. It is also clear that if it is pushed through the surface it will continue to present the same appearance until it has passed right through, when it will suddenly vanish away.

He would be unconscious of any movement on the part of the cube unless there was some difference between the first and last sections which he perceived.

If, for instance, the bottom face was red and the top face blue he would be conscious of a colour change on the part of the square which he perceived. It would start by being red and would pass through various shades of purple till, just before its final disappearance, it would be pure blue. But now suppose that it was pressed through his surface not "normally" but corner wise as indicated in Fig. 6—that is to say with one of its corners leading and one of its diagonals vertical. The plane being would then see quite a different set of figures. First would be a point; this would grow into a triangle which would increase in size until it reached a certain maximum when it would begin to develope three new sides at its corners which would grow, at the expense of the original sides, until a regular hexagon was produced when the reverse process would set in and the hexagon gradually change back into a triangle which in turn would dwindle away and disappear. It is easy to work out what would happen in the case of other solids, *e.g.*, Sphere, Cone, Tetrahedron, etc. All such changes would appear very mysterious to the plane being if he had formed no conception of three-dimensional space or the shapes of bodies therein.

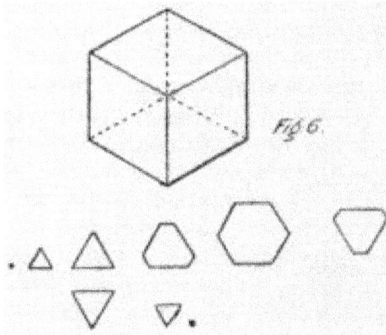

Fig. 6

Let us now extend this idea rather further.

Suppose we were to take a series of cinematograph pictures of the two-dimensional world, from the direction of the third dimension. We should obtain a succession of pictures each representing the precise state of affairs at some given moment in the two space world. Every thing in it would be represented in each. There would be no question of one thing being hidden by another because we are regarding them all from the direction of the third dimension in which they have an inappreciable extension. If we imagine the two space world to be very small or our camera to be very large there is no difficulty in supposing that each of our pictures includes the whole of the two space universe,—plane beings, earth, sun, planets, etc., all complete.

Imagine further that these pictures are reproduced, as cinematograph films actually are, on a transparent substance and then let us superimpose these successive pictures on one another in order so as to form a block. By this means we can represent the disposition of all the objects in a two space system at a number of successive instants in one single three space figure. For instance, the motion of a two space planet round its sun would become a part of a helix or spiral. If we now cut away from our block all the blank material which intervenes between the representations of the various two space objects we shall have a complete synthesis in three space of a succession of two space arrangements. If we were now to pass this three space object through a penetrable two space surface, *e.g.*, a soap film, we should exactly reproduce for the two space beings in it the changes which we had originally recorded.

By analogy we can see that it would be possible to account for all the changes in our three-dimensional space by supposing them to be due to the passage through it of suitably shaped and arranged four-dimensional solids, of which we only perceive at any moment a section whose extension in the fourth dimension is imperceptibly small.

It will appear later that I do not think that this is literally the case. The point I want to make here is that the phenomena of change or successive arrangement in space of a given dimensionality are capable of explanation in terms of forms in the next space higher, which latter do not change within themselves.

The precise import of this will appear when we come to consider the bearing of the higher space theory on the problem of the nature of Time.

CHAPTER II

THE SCOPE OF APPLICATION AND PROBABLE IMPORTANCE OF THE HIGHER-SPACE CONCEPTS.

In the preceding chapter I have tried to explain what is meant by the term "four-dimensional space" and to demonstrate some of its more important properties from the point of view of ourselves who live in space of three dimensions.

I am now in a position to state the basic hypothesis which I propose to discuss in the pages which follow.

Briefly stated it is this:—

"Higher space is a Physical reality and not a mere mathematical idea. In waking life the individual consciousness functions in a three-dimensional 'vehicle,' namely the physical body. But it may also possess at least one other vehicle—a four-dimensional one—and in this it may function after death and, possibly, during sleep, trance, anæsthesia and other forms of insensibility."

This hypothesis is not my own and I am not prepared to defend it as being necessarily correct. But, as I hope to show, there are a number of considerations which tend to support it and I do think it is sufficiently plausible to make it worthy of serious consideration before it is finally rejected by those who are students of these matters.

In this chapter I propose to deal with the different ways in which it is likely to prove of importance.

First of all, then, it has strong claims to be adopted as a working hypothesis by those who are students of Psychical Research, especially by those who are convinced of the validity of the Spiritistic explanation of communications purporting to emanate from the deceased.

Secondly, I believe that if accepted as valid it would do much to provide a common meeting ground for opposite schools of religious and scientific thought. Between these there was a most marked and unfortunate cleavage during last century and though there has been a very considerable rapprochement since the days when controversy was at its height there is still much to be done before we can hope for a complete community of thought and expression.

It is hardly necessary to say that these two spheres of application are very closely allied, but it is none the less convenient to separate them for purposes of discussion.

THE NEED OF A WORKING HYPOTHESIS IN PSYCHIC SCIENCE.

The studies of Psychical Researchers must necessarily cover a very wide area which is bounded on the one hand by Physical science proper, on another by Philosophy, on a third by Psychology and on a fourth by Religion. With each of these subjects it has close relations and yet possesses features which serve to distinguish it from any of them.

Sir William Barrett writes as follows of the scope of Psychical Research:

"The subjects to be considered cover a wide range, from unconscious muscular action to the mysterious operation of our sub-conscious self; from telepathy to apparitions at the moment of death; from hypnotism and the therapeutic effects of suggestion to crystal-gazing and the emergence of hidden human faculties; from clairvoyance, or the alleged perception of objects without the use of the ordinary channels of sense, to dowsing, or the finding of under-ground water and metallic lodes with the so-called divining-rod; from the reported hauntings of certain places to the mischievous pranks of poltergeists (or boisterous but harmless ghosts whose asserted freaks may have given rise both to fetishism and fairies); from the inexplicable sounds and movement of objects without assignable cause to the thaumaturgy of the spiritualistic séance; from the scribbling of planchette and automatic writing generally to the alleged operation of unseen and intelligent agents and the possibility of experimental evidence of human survival after death."

(*Psychical Research, p. 10*).

In view of the heterogeneous nature of this list I do not think it practicable to frame any hard and fast definition of Psychical Research. Moreover certain of the phenomena which it once studied—such as Hypnotism—have been largely taken over by "orthodox" science, and others, such as Telepathy and Clairvoyance, although of great intrinsic interest and some relevance, may ultimately be regarded as comparatively remote from the main body of psychic phenomena.

Roughly speaking, the characteristic feature of the latter is a suspicion, or *prima facie* appearance, or allegation that they emanate from, or are in some way connected with the activities of extra-mundane intelligences—notably the "spirits of" the deceased.

It is this feature which has caused their rejection by the sciences with which they would naturally appear to be associated and although our studies may in many cases show that the appearance is wholly spurious it must be remembered that, until every phenomenon is so disposed of and relegated to its appropriate "orthodox" science, the ultimate problem of Psychical

Research is largely a matter of the provision of answers to such questions as:—

"Is there any scientifically valid reason for supposing that Individual Human Personality survives bodily death?"

"If so, under what conditions does it persist?"

"What is the relation between these new conditions and those with which we are acquainted?"

Any investigation into Human Personality of a scope less than this can be included under the heads of Physiology or Psychology which are prepared to investigate any conceivable intricacy in the mental or bodily states of the living.

It is only when the investigator refuses to be limited by bodily death that Psychic science differentiates itself as a separate study.

I do not propose to consider here whether psychical research has yet given any satisfactory answer to the above mentioned questions or even whether there is any considerable chance of its ever being able to do so.

I merely wish to point out the nature of the problems with which it is concerned and which alone distinguish it as a separate science.

It follows that any hypothesis advanced with a view to co-ordinating the observed facts *may* find itself called upon to give an intelligible explanation of discarnate personalities, that is to say of human personalities not functioning through the flesh and blood bodies in which we are accustomed to meet them.

So far as our present knowledge goes and on the balance of all the available evidence I am inclined to think that this necessity is at least imminent.

The adoption of some form of working hypothesis is moreover imperative in the light of scientific history.

All who are interested in psychical research will agree that it is in the highest degree desirable that it should be recognised as a Science of a dignity commensurate with its intrinsic importance and on a level with the sciences more generally accepted as such.

That it has not, hitherto, attained this position in the eyes of the world in general is largely due to the fact that it has not yet fully reached that stage of development which chiefly distinguishes a science properly so called from mere speculatory observation.

This is no reflection on the many able and genuinely scientific men who have worked on the subject ever since it first became prominent in modern times some seventy years ago but is, on the contrary, a necessary and inevitable stage in the growth of any science whatsoever.

The processes of acquiring scientific knowledge are as invariable as those of logical thought. Just as all accurate reasoning may be reduced to a series of syllogisms, so the process of acquiring exact knowledge may be reduced to a series of analogous sequences.

These are:—(1) Observation.
(2) Induction.
(3) Deduction.
(4) Experiment.—A special form of observation.

I do not say that this sequence of operations is always consciously performed any more than when "thinking a thing out" we always consciously reduce our reasoning to its simplest syllogistic constituents.

But every time we acquire a new item of knowledge it would be possible to reduce the process by which we acquired it to a series of the sequences mentioned above.

It is worth while considering these steps in slightly greater detail.

OBSERVATION in the last analysis means no more than the recording and classifying of sensations, which are the only form in which we get any information as to the outer world.

INDUCTION means the process of concluding from a study of the observed and collected facts that there is some specific co-ordinating principle at work by virtue of which the facts exist. This is the process known as forming a working hypothesis.

DEDUCTION. In this stage we consider more closely the working hypothesis which we have formulated, and we conclude that if it be true certain other consequences must inevitably follow.

EXPERIMENT. This simply means that we turn again to the outside world and examine it to see whether these deduced results do actually obtain in practice.

If they do we argue that our hypothesis is, probably, a correct one and we retain it until it is shown that if it be correct some result must inevitably occur which in fact does not.

There is a difference between a *valid* hypothesis and a *true* one—or, as the latter is commonly termed, a Law.

Any hypothesis is valid which explains the observed facts or at least explains some of them and contradicts none. But the epithet "true" can only properly be applied when it has been shown that all necessary deductions are invariably borne out in practice. As a matter of fact we can never say this with absolute certainty for it is always conceivable that some exception may some day be found which would necessitate the remoulding of the hypothesis.

The most we can say is that certain hypotheses have stood the test in such a very large number of cases without a single failure that there is a very high degree of probability that they are really true.

The hypothesis that the Chemical "Atom" was the ultimate and indivisible unit of matter was a perfectly valid one in the light of the facts that had been observed at the time of its formation and of its apparent proof by Lavoisier and others.

It is only the facts which have been elicited by the study of Ionisation, of Radio-active substances and similar phenomena that have proved it to be untenable and necessitated the substitution of the electronic theory.

Again the Corpuscular theory of light affords a very pertinent illustration of the point I wish to make.

A number of facts regarding the phenomena of light were observed and classified and it was found that these could be explained by the hypothesis that light consisted of a stream of very minute particles moving at very high speed which impinged upon the eye and thus gave rise to the sensations observed. Up to a point this explanation was perfectly satisfactory and for a long time it held the field, partly because of the great prestige of Newton to whom much of its development was due and partly because it continued to explain subsequently observed facts without much straining.

But among other things it was demonstrated that in order to account for the observed phenomena of refraction it was necessary to suppose that the "Corpuscles" travelled faster in water than in air.

At first there was no means of determining directly whether this was so or not. But later the researches of Foucault made it possible to settle the point by direct measurement. When the velocity of light in air and water respectively was measured directly by Foucault's method it was found that the velocity in water was *less* than that in air. The Corpuscular theory was therefore untenable.

It is only by this process of forming, testing and, if necessary, rejecting hypotheses that we gradually attain to exact knowledge. As Prof. Richet says:

"La science n'a jamais été qu'une serie d'erreurs, approximations constamment evoluant constamment boulversé, et cela d'autant plus vite qu'elle était plus avancée."

(Annales des sciences psychiques, 1905, p. 15.)

From this brief resumé of the steps involved in scientific progress it is clear that the formation of a working hypothesis, by inductive reasoning from the observed facts, is a normal, necessary, and invariable step in the progress of any science whatsoever.

For this reason I do not think it likely that Psychical research will attain any widespread recognition as a science until it is in possession of a valid working hypothesis capable of explaining at least the more important of the observed facts. I believe that the higher space hypothesis fulfills this condition and if so it is clearly worth while adopting, purely provisionally and tentatively of course, by those who concern themselves with the subject.

I have said that I think that the conception of higher space has a bearing on the relations between Religious and Scientific thought.

I shall reserve for a later chapter the treatment of the question from the purely religious stand-point, and shall only examine here the reasons which seem to me to have led so many sincere and able scientific men to a position at variance with the religious and spiritual point of view.

This is, of course, closely bound up with the whole topic of the various attempts which have been made to satisfy the perennial demand for light on the mysteries of life and death and on the spiritual and non-material aspects of the universe.

It is out of the question for me to attempt to classify here the countless religions, sects, and philosophies which have arisen from time to time. But they do seem to fall into three main groups and although it is impossible to label these in any really satisfactory manner I think one may say that the Materialistic Scientists are the representatives of one school, the Orthodox Theologians of another, and the Occultists of a third.

By the Materialistic Scientists I mean those who see in matter or ether the ultimate and only permanent reality and who attempt to explain every experienced phenomenon in terms of matter and ether and of these only.

According to their view, Thought, Emotion, Consciousness, are no more than electro-chemical changes in the protoplasmic constituents of the brain cells. "The brain secretes consciousness as the liver secretes bile."

The idea of "spirit" is inconceivable to them; for the whole essence of Spirit is that it is not matter nor, so far as we can imagine, ether.

Now although this attitude is utterly repugnant to me, I can yet easily understand and sympathise with the state of mind which occasions it. I, too, feel that if there is one thing above all others to which one's intellect must cling at all costs it is the general proposition of the coherence and continuity of the universe—in other words the great Law of Causation. If ever we let go of that we find ourselves in chaos—which is insanity.

Within the "ring-fence," so to speak, of matter and energy the law holds good, but anything outside appears to the scientist as "discontinuous" and therefore, quite rightly, revolting. As against this point of view my contention is that it is quite possible to form an intelligible concept of Reality, different from and yet perfectly continuous with, the physical reality of the scientist.

This first purely materialistic school admits of fairly easy delimitation whereas the other two schools mingle together and diverge within themselves in so complex a manner that it is much more difficult to distinguish them from each other than to separate either of them from the first. But I think the difference is something of this kind. The school of which the Occultists are typical seem to me to tend to replace logically coherent explanation by mere descriptive nomenclature. On the other hand the Orthodox Theologians, while dogmatically asserting the existence of spirit and constantly emphasising the supreme importance of the spiritual life, are apt to ignore the intellectual demand for intelligible explanation altogether.

It is merely foolish to ignore or to ridicule on 'a priori' grounds the statements of those who claim to have investigated the problems with which we are concerned by the cultivation of abnormal or commonly latent faculties.

If such faculties exist, as is very possible, it is clearly no more than common sense that they should be exercised to the full in the solution of problems which present especial difficulties to the more normal methods of investigation. The results might be of the very highest possible value. Indeed, it may well be that the cultivation of such faculties is by far the best way of attacking the whole question. I am by no means prepared dogmatically to deny it. None the less I think we are entitled to expect that those who claim to have attained knowledge by these means should take some pains to make their results continuous with existing knowledge and to eliminate needless obscurities.

At present the application of the word "Science" to the utterances of the Occult schools—as commonly presented—is a complete misnomer.

In Theosophical literature, for instance, we are confronted with a scheme of things built up of such terms as "Astral Plane," "Etheric Double," "Causal Body," "Karma" and so forth.

With all due deference to my Theosophical friends I submit that this is not scientific explanation and cannot be so unless its exponents are prepared to tell us what is the relation between the astral plane and the physical world, between the etheric double and the body as known to physiologists.

Thus it is intellectually unsatisfying and little calculated to arouse the sympathetic interest of the strictly logical thinker.

I do not mean to say that none of the words of the type quoted have any real significance. On the contrary I think it very probable that many of them have and that they do represent real parts of the actual scheme of things. The trouble is that they are only names; and to name a thing is not the same as to explain it. In common fairness I ought, however, to admit that in several passages Mr. Leadbeater—one of the best known Theosophical writers— makes a distinct effort to escape from this tendency and it has further been opined by a very eminent Occultist that the bulk of contemporary literature on the subject will be out of date in a few years.

I am inclined to suspect that this failing was the cause he had in mind.

I repeat that my primary quarrel is not with the accuracy or otherwise of the statements made. Every word of them may be perfectly correct, but so long as they are expressed in terms wholly unrelated to pre-existing concepts I must, *qua* scientist, remain unconvinced.

The third school which includes the Orthodox Theologians sometimes resembles the Occultists in the use of unintelligible terms but their chief weakness is their failure to recognise and to cater for the intellectual demand for coherent explanation.

They never weary of insisting, quite rightly, on the paramount importance of Spiritual things, but no effort is made to show the continuity which must, in a sane Cosmos, exist between Matter and Spirit, or to state the "common factor," so to speak, which unites them as parts of a coherent whole.

For myself I refuse to believe that no such common factor is discoverable. As Sir Oliver Lodge says, "I have learned to believe in intelligibility."

This omission on the part of theologians did not so much matter in the days before Physical Science had attained to its present degree of development. Men knew so little about the material Universe that they experienced little difficulty in finding a place in it for Spirit and the Spiritual life. "Heaven" was conveniently represented as being somewhere "above" and "Hell" as somewhere "below." But now things have altered and we know quite a fair amount about the material world. Consequently the scientist demands—not unreasonably, I think—an explanation of "Spirit" which shall not conflict with the fundamental laws of continuity and causation.

So far the theologians have failed to meet this demand and to provide the necessary habitat for consciousness which shall be independent of, and yet causally continuous with, the material world which the scientist knows.

It is this illogical discontinuity which has alienated the sympathies of so many men of scientific mind and forced them to attempt to reduce all mental and spiritual phenomena to terms of matter.

The foregoing should be sufficient to show how important it is that Psychical Research—the connecting link between the study of the material and that of the purely spiritual—should adopt as soon as possible some form of working hypothesis which is not repugnant either to religious or scientific thought. It is only by doing this that we can hope to retain the sympathies of both classes of thinkers and this is surely worth an effort quite apart from all other considerations. Here again I believe that the higher space hypothesis meets the requirements of the case and this is my second chief reason for urging its adoption.

CHAPTER III

APPLICATION TO CERTAIN OF THE FACTS ELICITED BY PSYCHIC RESEARCH

In this chapter I propose to give some instances of the way in which the higher space hypothesis throws light on certain Psychic Phenomena which, without its aid, appear extremely obscure and difficult of explanation, but I shall make no attempt to cover the whole range of phenomena known to students.

Some are not yet, in my opinion, sufficiently well authenticated to necessitate consideration, and those which are, some—such as Telekinesis, Prevision, and certain aspects of unconsciousness—are more conveniently treated in later chapters; others are so mysterious as to render any attempt at explanation premature until we have a wider and firmer foundation of fact on which to build; others again, such as thought transference or Telepathy, will probably prove explicable without introducing the Higher Space hypothesis in any direct connection.

There are some, however, which may well be considered here.

The first, and by far the most important problem which confronts us in attempting to form an idea of post-mortem conditions, or of the existence of personality apart from the physical body, lies in the fact that we cannot conceive of personality as absolutely disembodied—as pure essence. Yet we know that if personality does in fact survive physical death, it must do so in some form, completely non-material in the ordinary sense of the word, which is invisible, impalpable, in short entirely imperceptible, to our normal senses.

Probably it is the difficulty of conceiving such a mode of existence which has chiefly prevented physical scientists, as a whole, from accepting the obvious interpretation of the evidence for Survival offered by various Psychic phenomena.

Few people, I think, who have studied the literature of the subject, would be prepared to deny that Survival is, at least, strongly indicated by the evidence in question.

But this difficulty of conceiving a state of existence, at once real and non-physical, has induced scientists to prefer to seek an explanation of the observed facts in terms of Thought transference, Secondary personality and so forth.[1]

But as soon as we introduce the concept of the Fourth Dimension this difficulty disappears.

We have but to suppose that after physical death the Individual consciousness is embodied in a vehicle organised, not from physical matter, but from Four-dimensional matter, *i.e.*, that which, in four space, corresponds to what we call "Matter" in three space.

Such a vehicle fulfills the required conditions in every way. It is scientifically real—that is to say, it has its habitat in a region as subject to law and as susceptible to mathematical analysis as the three dimensional world in which we at present live.

And yet it must be supposed to be, of its very nature, inapprehensible by our normal physical senses.

We are thus enabled to understand how those who have left this physical world may, although discarnate, be none the less as truly *alive* as ever, close to us and yet invisible, constantly in touch with us and yet beyond our normal ken.

This is the first and supremely important application of the hypothesis and it is impossible to over-emphasise it.

Of the more specific phenomena suitable for discussion here, I will first deal with Clairvoyance.

This is probably far from being a simple phenomenon of unvarying nature. There would appear to be at least four varieties and it is possible that as our knowledge of the subject increases we shall come to recognise still more.

The four at present distinguishable may be denoted as follows:—

(1) So-called "Etheric Clairvoyance." This is apparently no more than a heightening of the ordinary powers of vision.

(2) Perception of objects and contemporary events more or less removed in space from the percipient and invisible by ordinary means.

(3) Perception of non-material objects or events; as when a clairvoyant describes the appearance of a deceased person alleged to be present in "spirit form."

(4) Clairvoyance in time. That is to say the perception of future events—Prevision—or of past events—Postvision.

Instances of each of these four forms are abundant and amply verified except, perhaps, in the case of class 3 where verification is scarcely possible.

It is easy to understand how clairvoyance of the first type arises. We know that light consists of very rapid vibrations in the ether which impinge upon the retina and cause the sensation of sight. We also know that if a beam of white light is passed through a triangular glass prism it is bent aside and split up into the seven colours of the rainbow, viz., Red, Orange, Yellow, Green, Blue, Indigo, and Violet. The resulting band of colour is called a Spectrum. If the Spectrum so obtained is thrown upon a screen and a number of people are asked to mark thereon the limits of what they can see it will be found that these limits vary considerably.

We know, too, that there is a wide range of light-vibrations beyond the furthest of these visible limits, for although our eyes do not respond to them the photographic plate does. We also know that some of these vibrations will penetrate substances which are opaque to ordinary light although the opposite is the case for some substances. This is particularly the case with "ultra-violet" light which consists of vibrations more rapid even than those of violet light which are themselves the most rapid in all the visible spectrum. It seems reasonable therefore to suppose that certain people with abnormal retinæ or in an abnormal condition might be especially sensitive to these ultra-violet rays and that they might not only see things invisible to us but even see them *through* obstacles which are opaque to the sort of light to which normal eyes respond.

This explanation may serve for certain simple cases of clairvoyant vision but it soon breaks down because the visual image of any object seen in this way must be liable to confusion by the superimposed images of intervening objects.

Suppose for instance that a clairvoyant wishes to see, by this method, what is written on page 100 of a closed book. We will suppose that the covers and paper of the book are transparent to some kind of ultra-violet light to which the eye of the clairvoyant responds, whereas the ink is opaque to the same light.

On looking at the book the writing on page 100 would be visible all right, but so would that on the preceding 99 pages; it would, therefore, be practically impossible to read the 100th page.

It will be seen, therefore, that clairvoyance of this type must be of very limited scope and cannot be held to account for cases of the second type where the clairvoyant perceives events happening at a considerable distance, amounting in some instances to a matter of hundreds of miles.

I freely admit that at present I am not prepared to give an explanation of all cases where the distances involved are very large.

But to cases where the incidents or objects perceived are reasonably near the percipient, the higher space hypothesis offers a simple and elegant solution.

Consider the two dimensional analogue.

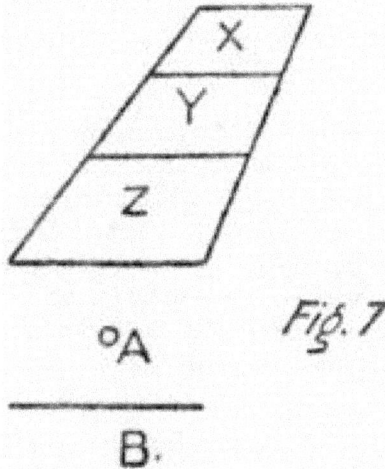

Fig. 7

Suppose that "A" Fig. 7, represents a two-dimensional observer and that X, Y, and Z are two-dimensional closed spaces, rooms, houses, or what not. The interiors of these closed spaces will be invisible to "A." All he will be able to see will be a straight line as at "B," for the boundaries of X, Y, and Z will be opaque and impassable to him.

But now suppose that he were to be lifted up vertically, out of the plane of the paper altogether. He would from this new position be able to see the interiors of X, Y, and Z, together with any two space incidents occurring therein. They would present approximately the appearance shown in Fig. 7 and the degree of foreshortening would diminish with the height to which he ascended above the plane of the paper.

In a precisely analogous manner we must suppose that three-dimensional obstructions do not exist for, and that the interiors of closed three-dimensional spaces are entirely open to, anyone who could regard them from a point situated in four space, i.e., removed from three space to a suitable distance in the direction of the fourth dimension. The greater this distance the less will be the foreshortening and the greater will be the range of vision.

There would be no question of intervening objects obscuring the view, simply because, in four space, three space objects do not intervene—the view of X in Fig. 7 is in no way obscured by the presence of Y or Z.

Compare with this the statements of many clairvoyants to the effect that when in the clairvoyant state they can, and do, see the front, sides, back, and every internal point of three space objects simultaneously.

The parallel is almost irresistible in its significance. Compare also the following case given by Professor de Morgan, and which is typical of the very numerous cases of this nature on record.

In this case the percipient was a little girl who was undergoing mesmeric treatment for fits by Mrs. de Morgan. While in the mesmeric state she was desired to follow Professor de Morgan mentally to the house at which he was dining and which was totally unknown to the child. The girl got there at once and gave an accurate description of the room in which the Professor was, the furniture which it contained, the people to whom he was talking and various small incidents which took place. On his return Professor de Morgan confirmed every detail of the description.

This is, of course, a very condensed resumé of the occurrence. Interested readers should consult contemporary Psychic literature which abounds with such cases. The point is that no amount of retinal hypersensibility will so much as begin to explain this sort of case, whereas it is not so utterly incomprehensible when we introduce the idea that the percipient may have been seeing four-dimensionally.

It is hardly necessary to observe that the sense organs involved cannot be the physical eyes. They must be supposed to belong to the four dimensional vehicle.

In attempting to explain this second type of clairvoyance along these lines, there seem to be two main difficulties involved and these are admittedly very great.

First, how is it that the four space vehicle possesses organs capable of perceiving three space objects and incidents? One would expect it to respond to four space impressions only.

Secondly, as soon as the distances involved become more than quite small it is very difficult to conceive how the percipient can simultaneously describe the events by the use of physical speech mechanism and also perceive them from a point of view which must be supposed to be very considerably removed in the direction of the fourth dimension.

A correspondent of my own who appears to possess this power of clairvoyance at a distance in a remarkable degree and to be able to exercise it at will, tells me that when she is seeing a distant scene, she is yet so closely in touch with her physical body that she is conscious of moving her hand, for example.

It is difficult to account for this on the four dimensional or any other theory.

I have no wish to minimise these difficulties or to claim that the introduction of the Higher space hypothesis clears up the whole matter. It does nothing of the sort.

But it does give us a dim inkling of what the general nature of the causes at work may be, especially as regards the power of "internal vision" mentioned above and which I particularly wish to emphasise.

This is more than can be said of any alternative theory with which I am acquainted.

Future study will probably show that this class of phenomena is far from simple and is really capable of being resolved into a number of sub-classes, each requiring its own appropriate explanation.

It is interesting to note that Mr. C.W. Leadbeater, the well-known Theosophical writer and clairvoyant, definitely introduces the four-dimensional concept in his book on Clairvoyance and ascribes the power of long-range perception to the intervention of what he calls an "astral telescope"; but there would appear to be no evidence in support of this idea beyond the *ipse dixit* of the writer and even he is very vague on the point.

The third form of clairvoyance, namely, the perception of non-physical things, is readily explicable on the hypothesis which we are considering.

Just as the physical body has sense organs adapted for the perception of physical things, so the four-dimensional body or "vehicle" will presumably possess analogous organs adapted for the perception of four-dimensional things.

In ordinary persons, we must suppose either that these organs are almost completely undeveloped, or else that the mechanism, whereby the impressions received are conveyed to the consciousness and recorded as memories, is defective or inhibited.

In the clairvoyant on the contrary we may suppose that they are well developed and active and that he is able consciously to perceive by their aid.

In advancing this explanation of the third form of clairvoyance, I do not wish it to be thought that I attribute an objective origin to all visions of objects which have no obviously physical reality.

Hallucination is often a *vera causa* and indeed it is comparatively seldom that we can eliminate it with certainty.

But I do not think it can legitimately be applied to all visions of this class.

The point is of some interest and worthy of a moment's thought even though it involves a digression from the main topic.

The essence of hallucination is that it should have a purely subjective origin and be unfounded on objective reality.

If I were to look round and find my sofa occupied by three green cassowaries playing nap I should, I think, be justified in assuming that I was the victim of an hallucination having no foundation in objective fact. It would, presumably, have arisen from a simultaneous excitation of the memory centres associated with the game of nap, cassowaries, the number three, and the sensation of greenness, occasioned, more or less fortuitously, by over-work or alcoholic excess.

On the other hand if I were to see the figure of an old man with a long white beard, one front tooth missing, shaggy eyebrows, black velvet smoking jacket, gold watch and chain, and so forth and were subsequently to find that such a person, answering the description in every detail, and previously entirely unknown to me, had really once lived, or was still living, then the view that this vision was the result of pure hallucination, would be untenable.

The probabilities against any chance stimulation of memory centres giving rise to precisely that combination of characteristics, are immeasureably large.

In such cases—and they are by no means unknown—we must attribute some degree of objectivity to the origin of the vision.

This is of importance in view of the tendency in some quarters to dismiss all such visions as purely hallucinatory.

We shall see later that the problems connected with Prevision and Postvision are also, if not completely explained, at least rendered less utterly incomprehensible by the introduction of the higher space hypothesis.

With the third class of clairvoyant phenomena is closely associated that group of facts known as "Phantasms of the Living, of the Dying, and of the Dead."

Certain aspects of the dream state, again, seem to be related to clairvoyance at a distance and are conveniently dealt with here.

Let us follow up the idea of a four-dimensional vehicle and see what light, if any, it throws on these questions.

Let us suppose that the four-dimensional vehicle becomes detached from, and loses touch with, the three-dimensional physical body during unconsciousness; or rather that unconsciousness is due to this detachment.

It follows that the "Ego" embodied in this four-dimensional vehicle can no longer receive impressions through the three-dimensional sense organs and that it is wholly dependent for communication with the outside world on those which belong to the four-dimensional vehicle. The nature of the impressions received will depend on the degree of development of these organs.

If they are completely undeveloped the Ego will be utterly oblivious of its surroundings, whereas if they are well developed the reverse will be the case and we may suppose the Ego to be as fully cognizant of the surrounding world as we are in ordinary waking life. It is interesting to compare with this the statements of those who claim to have consciously explored the "Astral plane" or four space world. They often describe sleepers as being present, but "in a brown study." Compare also the statement often found in communications purporting to emanate from discarnate personalities to the effect that, "We have seen so-and-so, but do not know whether he is dead or not."

Of course, it by no means follows that it will be possible, even under these latter conditions, to remember in waking life the impressions received during unconsciousness. On the contrary we should expect this to be the exception rather than the rule.

In their passage from sense organ to consciousness the impressions received will, *ex hypothesi*, not pass through the physical brain and the memory centres with which they become associated may be located in a position which is inaccessible to consciousness when embodied in the physical vehicle.

It would be possible, though not perhaps absolutely necessary, to account on these lines for the impression which most people have sometimes had, of apparently "remembering" a place which they have certainly never visited previously in waking life. They might, however, on this theory, have done so in sleep.

It would also account for those dreams in which the dreamer perceives an incident at a distance which is subsequently verified.

As for the ordinary chaotic dream, this, it seems to me may be accounted for in either of two main ways. If we suppose that the stimulation of certain cells (memory centres) in the brain causes an uprush into consciousness of the associated item of memory or "souvenir," it is not unreasonable to suppose that such stimulation is going on *in the body* all the time. But it will only be in the state, intermediate between profound sleep and waking, that these aroused souvenirs will, on the one hand get through to the consciousness— which in deep sleep is separated from the body altogether—and, on the other will escape over-ruling by the Will or obliteration by the influx of normal sensory impressions.

This would account for the fact that the majority of dreams appear to be of very short duration and to take place in the very act of waking.

The other cause of ordinary dreams is probably in its general nature suggestive. That is to say the Ego cut off from the outside world by the imperfections of its four-dimensional senses is quiescent, and in a state peculiarly favourable for the telepathic picking up of stray thoughts which suggest dreams.

This of course is especially the case when the dream is deliberately suggested by a hypnotic specialist, as is sometimes done.[2]

The subject of Phantasmal apparitions is also both complex in its varieties and obscure as to its causes.

The commonest explanation, namely, the telepathic influence of the percipient by the agent, does not seem to me to be applicable to every case. For instance, it is difficult to conceive how a man shot through the head can visualise himself sufficiently clearly at that moment to project a telepathic image of himself, including the wound, to the percipient. And, more generally, it is probable that few of us could visualise our own appearance with sufficient accuracy to do more than convey, telepathically, a vague general impression. On the other hand, if we are to suppose that the details are filled up, so to speak, by the percipient, how are we to explain accurate perception of clothing and so forth of which the percipient could have no knowledge?

Finally, the whole telepathic theory seems weak in this respect. If I in the act of death, vehemently long for, or think of, a certain person, it is clear that the thought in my mind which is most likely to be transmitted to the brain of a percipient will not be the thought of myself—still less of my own appearance—but rather of the other person. Why should this suggest *me* to his mind?

In experimental telepathy it is the idea on which the agent concentrated his mind that is transmitted to the percipient, not some other idea, and I see no reason for supposing that this is not always the case.

In cases where the apparition has been deliberately produced as the result of an act of will on the part of the agent, the apparition has invariably been preceded by the agent concentrating his mind on the person to whom he wishes to appear, *not* on himself.

In view of these considerations I frankly do not see how the telepathic theory can be unreservedly maintained.

When we add that in some of these experimentally produced cases the agent has himself seen the percipient and given details, subsequently verified, of the circumstances prevailing at the percipient's end; and then compare this with certain of the varieties of clairvoyance at a distance, we must surely admit that the supposition that the agent was really present, though not in the physical body, is by far the simplest explanation.

For cases of this sort the reader should consult "Phantasms of the Living." Some good selected instances are also given in "Death, it's Causes and Phenomena," by Messrs. Carrington and Meader.

The idea that conscious existence in a vehicle other than the physical body is possible even during life is borne out to some extent by the evidence of those who testify to having seen their own body, from outside, while in a state of unconsciousness. An interesting one is given in the above mentioned work. The narrator describes how as he lay in bed he felt a cold sensation creeping up his legs from the feet and gradually extending throughout his body. After this had gone on for some time he became momentarily unconscious and on coming to himself again "seemed to be walking on air" and to be entirely free from his body. He thought of a friend who was some hundreds of miles distant and in a few seconds he found himself in the presence of his friend in circumstances which he describes. His friend spoke to him but he could not stay. After much difficulty and perplexity he decided that he ought to return to his body and as soon as he had made up his mind on the point he found himself looking at his apparently dead body propped up in bed as he had been when this experience began. He tried to control it and in due course was able to do so and after a time successfully "re-embodied" himself apparently none the worse for his experiences.

The credentials of this case are good, and it is important to note that the friend referred to wrote spontaneously to say that he had seen the narrator at the time and in the circumstances which the latter describes.

For this reason it can hardly be dismissed as a mere hallucination or dream and it is relevant to the present discussion because the narrator saw his own body from outside and was apparently embodied all the time in a vehicle of some sort.

Another somewhat similar and equally remarkable case is given in the same work. This I shall deal with in a later chapter. In view of the foregoing considerations, I think it fair to say that the idea of a non-physical vehicle of consciousness capable, under the proper conditions, of temporary detachment from the physical body, has strong claims to be adopted as a working hypothesis for future investigations even though it is too early, as yet, to accept it as a proven fact.

It certainly seems to clear up certain cases of apparition and abnormal acquisition of information as to distant events, in a way which other theories do not do without being strained to an extent which I regard as unwarrantable.

It seems probable that the chief reason why such an hypothesis has not been adopted before is simply the difficulty of conceiving the nature of such a vehicle. But this is overcome if we suppose that it is four-dimensional.

The theory has, of course, its own attendant difficulties and I have no desire disingenuously to ignore them.

First it may be asked: How does the percipient see the apparition? For four-dimensional objects are, *ex hypothesi* invisible to three-dimensional sight.

Second: Why does the four-dimensional vehicle present the exact appearance of the three-dimensional body—clothes and all?

Third: How can it speak, *i.e.*, set up vibrations in three-dimensional matter, as it is sometimes recorded as doing?

It is admittedly far from easy to answer these questions, in the light of our present knowledge.

As regards the first, I should feel disposed to say that such apparitions would be the rule rather than the exception, were it not for the fact that only those whose four-dimensional organs are fairly well developed can see them. Even so it may be that they are only called into activity as a result of some special "rapport" existing between the agent and the percipient.

Professor Joire, in his book "Psychical and Supernormal Phenomena" points out that in nearly every case the percipient is in a state which he describes as "superficial somnambulism or passive mediumship" *i.e.*, in some condition which from the facts of Hypnosis we may consider to be especially favourable to the receiving of supernormal impressions of any kind.

This observation appears highly relevant and important.

The second difficulty may be met, though not, I must admit, in a particularly convincing manner, by supposing that the four-dimensional vehicle is so mobile and plastic, in respect to appropriate forces, that it is capable of being moulded by the mere power of will.

It would thus take the form which the agent commonly associated with himself, or which he observed his physical body to have after he had left it.

It would be possible to adduce a number of considerations in support of this view, but none of them are in any way conclusive and I therefore leave the reader to form his own opinion on the matter.

As regards the third point, there are two possible answers which might be offered.

On the one hand it might be suggested that the words heard are really objective; the result, that is to say of actual vibrations in the atmosphere, and that this result is produced because, in all such cases, the percipient is sufficiently mediumistic to provide the necessary material for the agent to "work up" some form of speaking apparatus. This is very difficult to conceive as possible, and yet we must suppose some such process to be involved in the production of the "Direct Voice," a phenomenon which, though baffling, seems well authenticated.

But this is rendered improbable by the cases where the speaking agent has been a living person, who records no such process as having taken place.

Besides, it is grossly improbable that a living person, or for that matter a newly 'dead' person, would know how to perform this operation.

The most probable explanation seems to be a combination of telepathic communication between the agent and the percipient accompanied by an auditory hallucination on the part of the latter. This would be, I think, quite natural.

These difficulties are much reduced, though not entirely removed, if we suppose that the agent is embodied, not in the four-dimensional vehicle, but in what, for lack of a better word, is called the "Etheric Double." This appears to be of a semi-material nature and is discussed at length in the chapter dealing with "The Connecting Link."

But this supposition would involve special difficulties of its own.

There is reason to suppose that the "Etheric Double," if it exists at all, is incapable of moving far from the physical body during life and it does not appear well adapted for use as a vehicle after death.

But on this point I shall have more to say later.

Generally speaking, it seems probable that no one of these explanations will be found to cover all the cases in question. But each is likely to prove applicable to some of them, although much careful investigation and analysis will be necessary before we can hope to be able to allot each case to its true cause with any degree of assurance.

None the less I am convinced that the hypothesis of a four-dimensional vehicle, detachable on occasion from the physical body, puts us, at least, on the right track.

I will now turn to the consideration of a series of phenomena which, from the point of view of the higher space hypothesis, are of far greater interest and significance than any we have yet considered.

I refer to the phenomena of "apport" and of "apparent penetration of matter by matter."

If we have a closed room, of which all the windows, doors, and other apertures have been carefully shut and sealed, it is clearly impossible to introduce any solid object into that room, by normal means, without breaking the seals and opening one of the apertures. The same would apply to a closed, locked and sealed box.

But the literature of Psychical research abounds with instances where objects are alleged to have been introduced into such closed and sealed rooms and boxes—or removed from them, which comes to the same thing—*without* breaking the seals. This is the phenomenon of "apport" properly so called and it forms a special case of the more general class of "apparent penetration of matter by matter."

Other cases of the latter are the tying of knots in an endless cord of such a nature that they can only be untied by breaking the cord or separating its previously sealed ends; or the passing, on to the wrist or ankle of some person or other, of a ring so small that it could not possibly be pushed on over the hand or foot.

A very good test would be the interlinking of two rings turned from different sorts of wood—as was attempted without success in the Slade-Zöllner investigation; or the passing of a piece of weldless drawn steel tube on to the middle portion of an ordinary wooden dumb-bell.

With regard to these phenomena I propose, first, to show in what their very great importance lies and then to discuss the nature of the evidence we have for their actual occurrence.

If the reader will refer back to the first chapter, he will at once perceive why I laid what must have appeared to be unnecessary stress on the fact that "rooms" and "boxes" which would appear to be absolutely closed to a two space being would be perfectly open to us who live in a three space world. Just as every point in the interior of a two space figure is absolutely open in the direction of the third dimension, so we must suppose from analogy that the interior of a closed three space figure—a box or room—is perfectly accessible from the direction of the fourth dimension.

Consequently on the hypothesis that four space actually exists as a reality, and is peopled by intelligent beings, possessed of the necessary "apparatus"—whatever that may be—the explanation of the phenomenon of apport is quite simple.

We have only to suppose that the object in question is moved out of the containing space, in the direction of the fourth dimension, and then put down again into three space outside the box or room in which it originally was. Or conversely, when it is a question of introducing an object *into* a closed space.

During transit, the object would, of course, be located entirely outside of three space.

I will not go at length into the question of how the tying of knots in an endless cord could be performed in four space. Any reader who cares to tie together the two ends of a piece of string for himself, will soon realise that it is not possible then to tie a simple knot in the string without untying the ends. If such an operation were to be performed, under test conditions, it would clearly be a case of apparent penetration of matter by matter.

Consider this case which is analogous to that of the steel tube and the dumb-bell suggested above:

Let A and B be two space objects. Fig 8. A two space being could not conceive of their being brought into the second position shown in the figure.

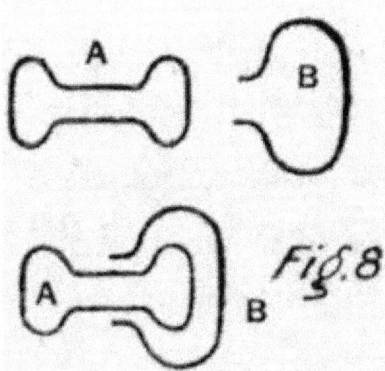

Fig. 8

But we, having the advantage of a third dimension of space could very easily pick up the object A and put it down in the second position with regard to B. Similarly a four space being of sufficient knowledge and manipulative ability could, theoretically, slip on to the middle part of the dumb-bell a piece of steel tube of a diameter too small to be passed over the two large ends. There are, of course, a large number of variations which could be introduced into this class of experiment but the foregoing will be sufficient to indicate their salient features.

For the purpose of detailed consideration I shall deal only with the case of the removal of a solid object from the interior of a closed and sealed box, which is typical of the whole of this class of phenomena.

Let it be clearly understood that at the moment I am not expressing any opinion as to whether this or any allied phenomenon has actually occurred. I am concerned merely with the inferences we should be compelled to draw if such an occurrence were substantiated scientifically beyond all possibility of doubt.

We have seen that given four-dimensional space as a reality and an intelligent four-dimensional being equipped with the necessary knowledge, powers, facilities and so forth, which I have included under the general term of "apparatus" the thing could be done in a comparatively comprehensible manner, although the actual manipulative details would still require clearing up.

The question now arises: Is this the only conceivable *modus operandi* that could bring about the same result? It is not. There is one other, and so far as I know only one other, theory which has been advanced to account for this type of phenomenon.

It has been supposed that the solid object in question is dissociated, by some obscure means, into ultra-atomic particles, is passed in this condition through the walls of the box and finally "integrated" again into its original form outside the box.

Now, apart from the obvious difficulty of imagining how these ultra-atomic particles are integrated into the precise form originally possessed by the object, this theory has at first sight a certain plausibility.

We know that all matter is probably susceptible of dissociation in a fashion that was originally supposed to be the exclusive property of Radium and other Radio-active substances.[3]

If, then, we postulate the existence of intelligent beings in a non-physical state of existence, there is nothing to prevent us from supposing that certain of them have acquired a sufficient knowledge of physical laws to enable them to effect a process of this nature artificially.

I do not say that this idea commends itself to me; but it is the explanation most commonly offered for the phenomena in question, and this fact taken in conjunction with its *prima facie* plausibility, entitles it to careful consideration before we dismiss it as untenable.

The real objection to it is a mere matter of Physics. The work of the scientists mentioned above goes to show that what we call matter is no more than a condensation of energy in the ether; and that the dissociation of matter is invariably accompanied by an enormous liberation of energy.

For calculations on this point the reader may refer to M. Le Bon's book "The Evolution of Matter."

Without going into such calculations it may be said that the amount of energy that would be liberated in the dissociation of a gramme of matter, would be amply sufficient, if it were produced in the form of heat, to fuse, and for that matter vaporise, the experimenters, the room, the whole house, and probably about half the town as well!

What becomes of this enormous quantity of energy which must be liberated during the process if the dissociation theory of the phenomena is correct? Why is its liberation not apparent, and painfully apparent, to the experimenters? How is it prevented from being dissipated and how is it collected again and recondensed into matter?

This point seems to me to be insuperable.

If the object within the box is dissociated, then energy must inevitably be liberated. If energy is liberated, then it cannot conceivably escape detection in such quantities.

I hope I have made my point clear. I am quite sure that any scientist accustomed to think in terms of energy will at once see the difficulty to which I allude.

I can see only one way out and that is to suppose that in some mysterious manner the liberated energy is stored in a "reservoir," so to speak, *which is not situated in our space at all,* and this at once lets us in for the original idea of a fourth dimension and higher space and all the rest of it.

Hence I maintain, and I think I have reason to maintain, that if these phenomena do actually occur at all, then we are compelled to admit that four-dimensional space does actually exist; and this no matter whether we accept as the proximate cause of the phenomena a simple four-dimensional movement or the far more elaborate and less satisfactory notion of dissociation and re-integration.

The reader will now understand why it is that I attach such great importance to these phenomena of apport and of the "apparent penetration of matter by matter."

If one of these phenomena could be established by absolutely incontrovertible experimental evidence, with the same degree of certainty, for instance, as the phenomenon of levitation without contact has been established by the recent researches of Crawford, I should regard the four-dimensional hypothesis as virtually proven.

I should be much interested to hear whether any interested reader can get out of the difficulty, assuming the authenticity of the phenomenon for the sake of argument, but I do not think that it will prove possible.

I will now pass to the consideration of the nature of the evidence that exists for the actual occurrence of this sort of phenomenon.

I will preface my remarks by two quotations from writers who appear to hold somewhat different views on the subject.

In "The Physical Phenomena of Spiritualism" Mr. Hereward Carrington says:

"Without now stopping to consider any *a priori* speculations as to the scientific possibility or impossibility of such a thing; the mere historic evidence in the case would certainly seem to point to the conclusion that fraud and nothing but fraud has been operative throughout and is quite sufficient to account for all the phenomena observed (save in the case of W.S. Moses, perhaps, that stumbling block to the rationalistic psychical researcher), in the presence of professional mediums.... In fact *all* these cases sift themselves down to the one primary consideration: could the medium, in spite of the searching, have introduced into the séance room, unseen by his sitters, the objects materialised."

It should be noted that the above refers to cases where the séance room is found, after the sitting, to contain objects which were certainly not there before. In this connection the last sentence of the passage quoted above is eminently justifiable and it is for this reason that I prefer to deal with varieties of the phenomenon which are more amenable to experimental control on the part of the experimenter; as for instance the removal of a solid object from the sealed box which we are considering.

Compare with this first quotation the following taken from Mr. Gambier Bolton's book "Psychic Force."

"During my sixteen years of experimental investigation into the question of the existence of this Psychic Force, the apparent penetration of matter by matter has been such a common occurrence at our experimental meetings, that unless this happens to take place in connection with some unusually large and ponderous object that is suddenly brought into our midst, or removed from the place where we are holding our meetings, I take but very little note of it. I could fill a large volume with instances where this has taken place in my own presence.... I am not engaged in an attempt to explain such things, but am merely recording phenomena which I myself have witnessed and which have been witnessed hundreds, nay thousands, of times by well-known investigators like Sir William Crookes and Dr. Alfred Russel Wallace under the strictest test conditions."

These two views are, to say the least of it, somewhat divergent. We must, therefore, see what is to be gathered from such original records as are available.

The *locus classicus* of this sort of phenomenon is the Slade-Zöllner investigation of 1877-9.

This investigation has received so much attention that it is impossible to avoid giving it somewhat careful consideration here.

Johann Carl Friedrich Zöllner was born in 1834. He was Professor of Physics and Astronomy at the University of Leipsic, a member of many learned and scientific societies and the author of a number of scientific treatises.

He was assisted, from time to time, in his investigations by Professors Weber, Fechner, and Scheibner all of whom were men of considerable eminence in one branch or another of mathematical or physical science.

The medium in whose presence the phenomena were produced was the well-known "Dr." Slade. This medium has been demonstrated to have resorted to fraud with a certainty that admits of no dispute.

But, as Mr. Hereward Carrington points out, we ought not to allow this fact to influence us in the consideration of any particular case. In the first place it is fairly certain that mediums who are capable of producing genuine phenomena under suitable conditions are also liable to resort to trickery when the genuine thing does not come off. (Cp. the case of Eusapia Palladino.) In the second, too great a reliance on antecedents is apt to produce an unreliable *a priori* prejudice. Every case should be considered on its merits alone and the medium's past history should only be allowed to influence our judgment if it can be shown that fraud has not been rigorously excluded and that the only argument against it is the argument from moral integrity.

In this case the argument from integrity is obviously inadmissible and as a matter of fact the precautions taken to guard against fraud were so very inadequate that we cannot accept the experiments in question as worth anything at all from the scientific point of view.

Zöllner's account of his experiments is to be found in his book "Transcendental Physics," translated into English by Mr. C.C. Massey in whom the author found an able and enthusiastic champion against his many critics.

Among the more important of his experiments were:

Production of knots in an endless string.

Slate writing under "test" conditions.

Disappearance and reappearance of solid objects.

Coins transferred from closed and fastened boxes.

Other instances of the apparent penetration of matter by matter.

The careful study of this book is of the greatest value as an exercise in the criticism of evidence and as a guide for anyone who proposes to study such matters at first hand.

I do not think that I can illustrate my meaning better than by a description of my own impressions in connection with the book.

When I first read it I was much impressed by the scientific eminence of those who bore witness to the authenticity of the events described.

I reflected that here we had a Physicist of no mean order, assisted by other scientists of European reputation, men trained, presumably, in the art of exact observation and not likely to be deceived by the manipulations of a conjuror. Surely we must believe their testimony if we are to assign any value to human evidence at all!

Then, as I thought over the matter more and became more convinced of the importance of the conclusions to be drawn from these experiments, if genuine, I felt that these considerations, although possessed of their own importance, were yet not sufficient to warrant acceptance of the evidence without careful examination of the intrinsic qualities of the latter.

On further study of the book I was struck by the fact that not one of the special experiments, carefully designed by Zöllner to establish the genuineness of the phenomena and the validity of the four-dimensional explanation beyond all doubt, had succeeded. This was suspicious, although not, of course, conclusive. Specially devised test experiments may very likely fail simply because they may involve the upsetting of some essential condition which is not fully understood by the experimenter. But when such experiments fail, while others of, apparently, identical general nature succeed, it gives one cause for thought.

Finally, when I came to examine the records of individual experiments in the light of the criticisms of Mr. Carrington, of Dr. Hyslop and others, I realised that the nature of the evidence was emphatically *not* good enough to justify our accepting as demonstrated the facts which Zöllner claimed to have established.

I shall not waste my own time and that of the reader by giving numerous instances of the sort of thing I mean.

I will confine myself to the case that we are more especially considering as being typical of the whole of this class of phenomena, *i.e.*, the case of the removal of a coin from a closed and fastened box.

Zöllner describes how in December 1877 he put some coins in a small cardboard box and had closed it by glueing a strip of paper round the sides. He had done this in the expressed hope that Slade might be able to remove them and thus give a proof of the reality of the fourth dimension which was Zöllner's pet hobby. In May 1878 Slade came again to Leipsic and performed the feat, at any rate to the satisfaction of Zöllner.

The box was put on a table together with some slates and other objects and Slade and Zöllner and his colleagues sat round. Zöllner satisfied himself by shaking the box that the coin was still inside and in answer to Slade's enquiries explained the purpose of the experiment and its importance if successful. There was a little preliminary slate writing and then Slade began staring into a corner of the room and saying "I see funf and eighteen hundred seventy six." Then a hard object was heard to fall on the slate which Slade had held under the table all the time and on withdrawing the slate it was found to be a five mark piece of date 1876. Zöllner then snatched up the cardboard box and shook it only to find that it was empty.

This is a very highly condensed description of the proceedings but I do not think I have been guilty either of "*suggestio falsi*" or of "*suppressio veri*".

Interested readers can refer to the original.

Now, if Zöllner had been writing no more than a casual account of a well-known experiment, inserted for the sake of completeness or for similar reasons, it would be well enough.

But to offer his account, in the face of a very natural scientific incredulity, as a conclusive demonstration of a highly controversial point, was an insult to one's intelligence.

There are numerous criticisms that might be made, but I shall confine myself to pointing out only the more conspicuous of them.

In this experiment there are two main methods by which the result might have been obtained by fraudulent means.

There seems no doubt that the coin was really in the box at the beginning of the sitting. We may equally accept the statement that the box shaken at the end of the experiment did not contain a coin.

On the hypothesis of fraud, therefore, one of two things must have happened.

Either Slade must have contrived, during the sitting, to possess himself of the box, open it, abstract the coin, close the box again, and return it to the table; or else he must have substituted for the box, which at the beginning of the sitting contained the coin, another (empty) box, previously prepared to resemble the original.

I do not think the former method to be at all likely.

One cannot unstick a length of glued paper and stick it up again in a few seconds unobserved.

On the other hand everything lends itself to the supposition that the second method was actually adopted.

In the first place we know that the box was prepared some six months previous to the experiment.

It is true that Zöllner is a trifle hazy as to dates, saying at the outset that Slade's first visit to Leipsic was in December 1877, and, later, that the first and second visits were in November and December 1877.

But this is comparatively immaterial, the point being that Slade had presumably had ample time and opportunity for finding out all about these boxes and for preparing substitutes. I say "presumably" because in the absence of definite evidence to the contrary, we have no reason to suppose that these boxes were kept in an inaccessible place or that Zöllner had never mentioned his intentions with regard to them to Slade himself or to anyone else. I consider then that so far as the records go, we are perfectly entitled to suppose that Slade was able to prepare, and, in fact, actually did prepare, an empty counterfeit box, externally similar to that prepared by Zöllner. The second, and almost incredible, point to be noticed is that apparently no steps of any sort were taken by Zöllner to identify either the box or the coin after the sitting with those originally prepared by him.

In fact, he definitely says that he had completely forgotten, indeed had never so much as observed, the value or dates of the coins used!

With such gross carelessness in the control, the trick becomes exceptionally easy to perform.

Slade goes to the séance armed, among other things, with an empty, counterfeit box resembling Zöllner's, also with a five-mark piece of the right date—I think that even Zöllner would have been suspicious if the coin that fell on the slate had been dated 1878! Zöllner shakes *his* box—the genuine one—and satisfies himself that the coin is really there. Then follows a little preliminary play with the slate and so on, the simplest matter in the world to an artist like Slade. At the critical moment Slade diverts the attention of the experimenters from the table by the world-old conjuror's dodge of gazing fixedly in some other direction and murmuring "I see—see—funf," etc. While Zöllner and his colleagues are glancing in the same direction to see what he is looking at, Slade swiftly substitutes his counterfeit box for the original, and the trick is to all intents and purposes done. All he has now to do is to drop the coin which he brought with him on to the slate at any convenient moment and draw out the latter in triumph!

Given the astounding guilelessness of Zöllner and the complete lack of control revealed by the records, the thing was absurdly simple.

And yet Zöllner refers to it as having been performed under "such stringent conditions!"

The foregoing example will, I hope, make quite clear how much importance I attach to the Slade-Zöllner investigations.

I am not prepared to say that Slade never produced genuine phenomena, either with Zöllner or with anyone else.

On the contrary, I think it probable that he possessed a certain amount of genuine mediumistic power which, however, he did not hesitate to supplement by cheating when occasion offered.

Some, or for that matter all, of the Slade-Zöllner experiments may happen to have been genuine. But in view of the known untrustworthiness of Slade and the complete lack of proper scientific control revealed by a study of the published records we must write them off as quite valueless from a scientific point of view.

I have dealt with this particular case at some length partly on account of the vehemence of the controversies which have raged round it and partly because the discrediting of Zöllner's observations has done much to bring the whole idea of the fourth dimension into disfavour and even into ridicule. This, I feel, is unfair and I wish to make it clear that my present advocacy of the claims of the higher space hypothesis is in no way based on the Zöllner experiments.

There are, of course, in the literature of the subject a large number of other cases which are not so obviously unreliable—some, in fact, which are distinctly good.

Dr. S.A. Peters gives an account of an early experiment by Dr. Hare—one of the pioneer investigators—in which two small balls of platinum were transferred to the inside of two hermetically sealed glass tubes. It is not a bad case but is a very old one and the record gives no particulars of any special precautions taken to exclude fraud.

The Milan Committee appointed to investigate the mediumship of Eusapia Palladino failed to obtain any confirmation of Zöllner's experiments, but they seem to have been puzzled by an unaccountable incident where the medium managed to get into, or partially into, a coat while her hands were being held by the Committee. I do not myself regard this case as convincing.

The American Society for Psychical Research recorded some observations with a Mrs. Roberts of New York, who managed to liberate herself from a carefully made and sealed cage which was closed and sealed by members of the investigating committee. I do not know anything at first-hand about the credentials of this case. Dr. Paul Joire quotes it and I suppose, therefore, that he considers it reliable.

The same author also quotes at length a case observed by Dr. Pogorelsky and other Russian investigators with the medium Sambor. In this case a cane chair was passed on to the arms of two of the experimenters whose hands were clasped and bound together. That is to say, whereas to start with the chair was by itself and independent of them it was, at the end of the proceedings, found suspended from their arms by the opening at the back. As the opening was too small for either of them to have wriggled through even if they had wished to do so this was a clear case of apparent penetration of matter by matter.

The evidence in this case seems to be well above the average although it cannot be said to amount to mathematical certainty.

Mr. Gambier Bolton gives a distinctly good case in his book "Psychic Force," p. 65. Under exceptionally favourable conditions he observed the removal of a light table from a sort of tent which he had constructed and very carefully closed and secured. This is one of the best cases I know; it took place in the observer's own room, it was done impromptu, it was well observed in light, and all the objects concerned were the observer's property and not of a kind to admit of prestidigitation. It is difficult to see any way out of it and yet I must confess that I am not wholly satisfied. I feel that in every case there is just something more needed to carry complete conviction and I should very much like to see a good case myself.

Other instances are common. The records of the mediumship of Stainton Moses, for instance, abound with them. But as there were never any test conditions imposed, so far as I am aware, it follows that the question of the genuineness of the phenomena is simply a matter of the integrity of the medium. On this point every reader must be left to form his own opinion. Many authorities have professed the greatest confidence in Moses. Mr. Podmore, on the other hand, presents the suspicious features of the case in a very able criticism in his "Modern Spiritualism." Anyway on a point of such importance as this I do not think it would be right to allow the matter to be settled by any purely moral considerations of the type adduced in the case of Moses.

In general, then, I should say that the phenomena of the apparent penetration of matter by matter are not established with the same degree of certainty which characterises certain other phenomena, and which we ought to demand before accepting them as scientifically proven or utilising them without reserve as a basis for the construction of theories.

In the interests of the science it is in the highest degree important that experiments of this nature should be carried out under real test conditions.

Should any of my readers be so fortunate as to be acquainted with any medium capable of producing these very rare phenomena with regularity, I should esteem it a great favour if they would kindly inform me. I would very much like to arrange some definite experiments to settle the matter—if possible once and for all.

There is one other direction from which, in my opinion, we receive a strong hint that four-dimensional space is intimately connected with Psychic phenomena.

I refer to Crawford's work on table levitation. This investigation is undoubtedly destined to take rank as a "classical" research of the first magnitude and no one who professes to take an intelligent interest in the scientific and experimental aspects of Psychic investigations can afford to be without his book.[4]

In a later chapter I shall have occasion to refer to certain aspects of his results and to show how they fit in with those of other investigators working on very different lines.

In the present context I propose only to call attention to the rigidity of his "cantilever," a phrase which perhaps needs some explanation.

As a result of the most careful and painstaking researches extending over a period of nearly three years and performed under conditions which were singularly favourable for observation, he has been enabled to arrive at certain definite conclusions as to the mechanical causes of telekinesis in general and table levitation without contact in particular.

He finds that when the table is lifted clear of the floor it is supported by a definite structure or cantilever. This structure is invisible and impalpable, or nearly so, and appears to be organised out of some form of matter actually taken from the body of the medium.

Dr. Crawford has been able to work out the form and size of this structure with considerable accuracy. For the details of method and results the reader should consult his book. It is possible to pass a thin rod through this structure in any direction without causing a breakdown, and without encountering any perceptible resistance.

Nevertheless the structure can resist compressional, tensional and torsional stresses of very considerable magnitude as I am able to testify from personal experience.

I may mention here that I have witnessed these phenomena myself under good observing conditions and that I am prepared to certify in the most unequivocal manner that they are absolutely authentic; that is to say the result neither of fraud—conscious or unconscious—nor of illusion.

Indeed, I do not suppose that an intelligent person could suppose them to be due to anything of the sort after a careful study of Dr. Crawford's book, quite apart from any personal observation and I only add my own testimony as a small make-weight for what it may be worth.

We are here confronted with a sort of mechanical paradox. How can we conceive that the structure manages to combine the contrary attributes of rigidity and impalpability? Rigidity means simply the power of resisting deformation under stress. That is to say that in order for a body to be rigid it must be capable of developing within itself forces which shall counteract those which tend to deform it. If we apply a stress—a deforming force—to a rigid body, then this force must be met by some opposing force; otherwise the body will be deformed. Normally this is a matter of molecular cohesion, etc.

Now, this structure resists deformation under stress, and it therefore follows that the deforming forces must be counteracted by opposing forces.

But the structure is impalpable, and we can pass a rod through it in any direction without encountering any resistance.

This being so it is difficult to conceive how the forces resisting deformation can be applied from any direction in which we can move the rod, *i.e.*, from any direction known and accessible to us.

The more one tries to think out what is involved in the idea of an impalpable and yet rigid structure, the more hopeless it seems.

But I think that the concept of four-dimensional space will help us even here.

We know two things. First that the structure is rigid and therefore that the deforming stresses are counteracted by opposing forces and, second, that these opposing forces are apparently not applied from any direction with which we are acquainted. But is it not possible that they may be applied from some direction with which we are *not* acquainted?

From some direction, in fact, of which the hypothetical fourth rectangular axis of space is a component.

Is it possible that the matter which is drawn from the body of the medium, and which forms the structure, is composed of molecules whose atoms are arranged not in space of three dimensions but in space of four dimensions?

I do not say that this is necessarily so; but I must confess that to me it looks rather like it. Still less am I prepared to say that the atoms are arranged four dimensionally. We do not know enough for that yet. But it is, I think, a possibility, although for all I know to the contrary there may be many other ways in which forces operating in four space might act on three-dimensional atoms and molecules.

Consider a two-dimensional analogy again.

Imagine a number of flat-headed drawing pins lying points upward on a flat surface. Taken collectively as a system they will have no rigidity. Now imagine a board pressed down on those points so that they penetrate into the board. The points and the board alike will be invisible to the two space beings inhabiting the surface and yet the drawing-pins, taken collectively as a system would have acquired rigidity. Deforming stresses would be resisted by cohesive forces operating outside the two space surface altogether.

This analogy is, naturally, imperfect; but I think that it enables us to form some idea of the way in which the rigidity of the levitating structure might result from its being held together by binding forces operating outside our space.

The only alternative is to suppose that the particles of which the structure is composed are rendered rigid by virtue of some peculiar motion of the ether of a nature entirely unknown to us and different from any type of ethereal motion with which we are at present acquainted. This is palpably unsatisfactory and has the grave defect, in an explanation, of failing even to begin to explain.

In an article published in "Light," for July 14, 1917, I discussed this point in somewhat greater detail.

This is all that I have to say with respect to the phenomena which are essentially "Psychical." In the next chapter I shall deal with two other applications of the theory to more general questions.

FOOTNOTES:

[1] Far be it from me to suggest that these last-mentioned factors play no part in the phenomena. On the contrary, their effect is at least very considerable, and does much to obscure and complicate the work of interpretation.

[2] NOTE.—The foregoing remarks on the subject of Dreams might be taken to imply an ignorance of the views inaugurated by Freud, and extended by Jung, Pfister, and others of the Psychoanalytic school. But I do not think that there is any fundamental contradiction involved. Even if, as this school tends to maintain, there is no dream without it's hidden and esoteric meaning, it is still perfectly legitimate to suppose that the *form* which a dream takes may be determined by causes of the type which I have been discussing here. These would provide the raw material so to speak which would be worked up into the finished dream in accordance with Freudian principles.

[3] Compare the recent work of Rutherford, Soddy, Le Bon and others.

[4] "The Reality of Psychical Phenomena" (Watkins).

CHAPTER IV

SOME OTHER POSSIBLE APPLICATIONS OF THE HYPOTHESIS

In this chapter I propose to deal first with the questions of Time and prevision and in the next to show how the higher space ideas help us to clear up certain difficulties in connection with Vitality and Will.

The question of the nature of time is one which brings us into close contact with Philosophic and Metaphysical thought and one is apt to find oneself in very deep waters indeed. Still I think it is possible to show how the higher space ideas come in without involving myself in controversial statements. I shall leave it to others to decide whether, as I am inclined to suspect, the acceptance of higher space concepts as actualities would provide Metaphysicians with a somewhat new field of speculation or modified methods of expression.

It has been suggested by some writers that "the fourth dimension is time."

At first sight this definition would seem to conflict with our original statement that it is an unknown direction in space at right angles to every direction which we can find. But, as a matter of fact there is a certain amount to be said for the idea. It might be pointed out, for instance that for an object to exist at all it must possess some "extension" in time. It must, that is to say, not only possess a certain length and breadth and thickness but must also exist for a certain time. Otherwise it simply does not exist. Then, again, if we were able to "travel" in time we might fairly claim to be travelling in a previously unknown direction, different that is from any direction at present known to us.

Moreover, as I showed at the end of the first chapter, changes in our space could be accounted for by supposing them to represent our perception of a series of parallel sections made by our three-dimensional space cutting an assemblage of suitably shaped and arranged four-dimensional solids. It is here that I think we find a clue which may perhaps be relevant to the present discussion.

I am far from being prepared to say that the fourth dimension *is* time because I doubt whether time as commonly understood is an "absolute" thing. It seems to me to be rather a limitation of our finite consciousness.

In the Divine Consciousness which I take to be alone Absolute there can be, surely, no Past or Future; all must be comprehended in the Eternal Now.

But I do think it possible that if we were not limited to three dimensions in thought and experience we might be able greatly to modify our present conceptions of time and to understand many things with regard to it which at present appear obscure.

Let us start by considering for a moment our ordinary idea of "Time." To start with we associate it with clocks and next, if we go a step further back, with the movement of the earth relative to the sun and stars. A clock is merely a mechanical device for subdividing into equal parts of suitable size the intervals between successive recurrences of certain astronomical events. In fact our ordinary ideas of time are determined by a wholly fortuitous arrangement of the component parts of the Solar System. If the masses etc. were other than they are, our day and year would be altered accordingly. It is quite conceivable that in some highly complex system of several "suns" moving under the influence of their mutual attractions and attended each by its own sub-system of satellites, there might be a world from which all the observable astronomical phenomena would be so complicated that its inhabitants could detect no regularity in them at all.

If, for instance, any given astronomical grouping of the observable bodies only recurred once in a hundred generations of the inhabitants, the measurement of time from astronomical data would be scarcely practicable.

A similar state of things would result if the average life of a man on earth lasted about ten minutes.

Again we know that the regularity of the changes in our system is really only apparent, for all the motions by which we habitually measure time are gradually altering under the influence of tidal friction.

So we see that all our ordinary ideas of time are based on the fissiparous assumption that certain distributions of matter will occur regularly; that is to say in such a manner that if we could observe any two successive cycles simultaneously they would appear coincident.

The same can be shown to apply to any other system of time measurement which we can substitute for the observation of astronomical phenomena.

This is so because, apart from all other reasons, every conceivable method must be based on the assumption that the properties of matter are invariable. But these seem to be functions of the properties of ether and since the solar system is certainly, and the whole universe probably, moving through ether-filled space, this means that our methods of time measurement must ultimately be based on the assumption that the ether is homogeneous.

Very probably it is; but there is no reason why it should be—on *a priori* grounds.

Now M. Bergson has been at pains to discriminate between this time "of succession" which we know and true time—the time "of duration." His view, as I understand it, is that the succession of events or "spatial simultaneities" by which we *measure* time no more *is* time than the succession of marks on a foot-rule *is* the material which we measure with it.

What we actually experience as time does not necessarily correspond with the spatial recurrences which measure it.

We all of us say, when we are bored, that "the time passed slowly" or, when we are happy and amused, that "the time flew" and although this may appear at first sight to be no more than a loose way of speaking I think that there is more in it than that. It is here, in fact, that we find what I can only call a "check" on the measurement of time.

It is the apprehension of something capable of undergoing change, of Psychic states to wit, whose changes are yet totally independent of the spatial changes by which we ordinarily measure time. A man who is hanging by a frayed rope over a precipice waiting for someone to come and rescue him might very likely say that "It seemed hours" although it might really have been no more than a very few minutes.

Yet in one sense he might be speaking the literal truth. The changes which took place in his mental states during those few minutes might well be as complex and extensive as those he would normally experience in the course of hours.

This should suffice to make clear the difference between the "real time process" which we measure and the recurrence of spatial simultaneities by which we measure it.

If we consider the latter alone we soon find that they are difficult of comprehension. As Mr. Lindsay says in his book "The Philosophy of Bergson," p. 128.

"If we eliminate real time altogether we get a number of simultaneities whose relation to each other we cannot understand.... For the relation between the simultaneities is taken to be that of the parts to the whole, but ... that is itself a simultaneity ... the relation of the simultaneities which are now taken as in their aggregate constituting change must be conceived of as necessary, as somehow all existing at once."

And again:

"We can only understand change by realising that it is incapable of spatial expression...."

This quotation seems to me to be important because it brings out clearly the points with regard to which I think that the higher space hypothesis may be important.

For although I am entirely in accord with the idea that there are, so to speak, two sorts of time I feel that in the light of the hypothesis we cannot allow the statement that "change is something which is incapable of spatial expression" to pass unchallenged.

If it were put in the form, "material change is incapable of expression in terms of space of three dimensions," I should have nothing to say.

But in the course of my remarks on the phenomena of change in a two-dimensional world, I pointed out that it is possible to integrate an infinite number of three-spatial simultaneities into a four-dimensional whole.

The introduction of this concept seems to me calculated to modify the whole aspect of the question.

For, by its light, we see that all the three-spatial simultaneities by which we mark time *can* exist at once.

They can do so because the arrangement of material particles which constitutes a given simultaneity may be regarded, if we so wish, as a thin section of a four dimensional solid.

We can say, then, that there are two sorts of time.

First there is ordinary Physical "time" which is measured by the recurrence of three-spatial simultaneities and this, if we choose, may be regarded as produced by the passage across our space of something which has extension in four dimensions.

Secondly, there is what I am inclined to call Subjective time, consisting of changes in Psychic states; and which may be regarded, provisionally, as being perceived by virtue of changes in "objects," including the vehicles of our own consciousnesses, in space of four dimensions, or, at any rate, in space of a dimensionality higher than three.

I do not mean the foregoing remarks to be taken too literally for I do not regard three-dimensional change as produced by the passage across our space of actual four-dimensional solids. This seems to me to be altogether too crude an idea and was only introduced to bring out my point that three-dimensional change is *capable of expression* in terms of four space.

Whether it is solely a phenomenon of consciousness or whether there may be something in the nature of four-dimensional "lines of force" which cut three-dimensional space and determine material distributions I am not at all prepared even to surmise.

A side light on this matter of the two sorts of time is given by the phenomena of time in dreams. It is well known that we may be awakened by a noise and that in the very few seconds between the occurrence of the noise and our becoming completely conscious we may experience a long and complicated dream in which we may do and say things which would take quite a long time in actual life and this without any sense of hurry.

This seems to show that the "time scale" for the dream state is not the same as that to which we are accustomed in our waking hours. The difference should be sought, as Mr. Bragdon points out, in the differing vehicle of consciousness.

This idea can be pushed much further.

I have suggested that there is a sort of time which is, so to speak, peculiar to our space and which is expressible in terms of four space; and that there is another sort of time which appertains to four space itself, associated, that is, with four space change in the same way that three space time is associated with three space change.

But if we accept the idea that there are more dimensions of space than three we cannot refuse to consider the possibility that there are more than four. If so we must say that four space change is in turn expressible in terms of five space in just the same way that three space change is expressible in terms of four space.

Now, it is evident that a being embodied in four space and possessing, either temporarily or permanently, no three-space vehicle, will be unaffected by three space change and will, therefore, be independent of three space time. Four space change would take the place of the three spatial simultaneities by which we, embodied in three space, reckon time, and five space change would take the place of the changes in Psychic states which for us give rise to the second aspect of time which we have been discussing.

The whole dual nature of time would be repeated but with the difference of being one dimension higher.

The same may be applied to five space and six space and so on, indefinitely.

In each case the changes giving rise to the experience of subjective time would presumably be the resultant of the changes of all spaces higher than that of the lowest vehicle, but that of the next higher space would predominate.

Hence Consciousness could never be altogether free of the experience of time until it was embodied only in the highest space of all, which we must suppose to possess the attributes of infinitely dimensional space.

And this will only apply to the Divine Consciousness.

All this is admittedly highly speculative but seems to me the natural deduction if we assume the existence of spaces of dimensionality higher than four.

The nature of maximally dimensional space is a question which I do not propose to discuss here as it is somewhat conspicuously outside the sphere of practical politics. For other observations on this subject, including some remarks on the concept of "curved time," the interested reader may profitably refer to Mr. Bragdon's book "Four Dimensional Vistas."

Mr. Klein treats the question in a rather different, but highly interesting, manner in his book "Science and the Infinite."

PREVISION.

The subject of prevision is obviously closely allied to that of time, since the only considerable difficulty lies in the fact that the incidents forseen are removed in time. They are wrapped in the darkness of the future and we say that they "have not happened yet."

There are two forms which an attempt to explain the fairly numerous good cases of prevision may take.

One way is to say that the future is latent in the present in that it is determined by factors at present in existence. The other is to say that there is no such thing as Past or Future, but that both are comprehended in the Now and that it is merely on account of the limitations of our Consciousness that we cannot apprehend them.

According to the former view the power of prevision is the result of a mere heightening of the faculties by which we can always foresee the future to some slight extent. If we see a blind man walking towards the edge of a cliff it is not difficult to foresee that he will, probably, fall off it and be smashed at the bottom. Such a sight could easily be supposed to give rise to a visualisation of the corpse at the bottom of the cliff, which might pass for a prophetic vision.

In such simple matters it is not difficult to imagine that a suitable clairvoyant state, combined with unconscious but accurate reasoning and subsequent visualisation, would enable the percipient to forecast the future.

But clearly the accuracy of such a forecast would depend on the perception of *all* the factors involved, as well as on the precision of the unconscious reasoning.

Hence, although we might readily accept this explanation in the case of prevision of events in the immediate future, or in the case of vague presentiments, it becomes increasingly difficult to do so, as the event prevised becomes more remote and the number of factors which may possibly influence the issue are proportionately increased.

I need hardly say that these factors of which I speak must include Psychic states and so forth.

To use the terminology to which we have by this time become accustomed, we could, theoretically, forecast the distribution of every particle of matter in three space, provided we knew present distribution and velocities; and provided also that no interference could arise from external, *i.e.*, four space, sources. But in order to be certain of the latter, we must know all about four space dispositions and so on to the "N"th degree.

Absolute prevision could therefore only result from a complete knowledge of all the factors in *every* space combined with absolutely perfect reasoning powers.

Although, as will be seen, certain of the ideas in the above have a place in what I believe to be the true theory of prevision, the explanation as above described does not appear to me to be satisfying.

The heightening of faculty required in all but the very simplest cases is too great to be accepted except in the last resort.

Now, as regards the other theory, that the future does actually exist *now* and that only our own limitations prevent us from apprehending it.

Consider again the crude and metaphorical representation of change as resulting from the passage across our three space of a congeries of four space solids which supposes that the distribution of matter at any moment is simply a very thin cross section of this congeries.

If this were the case it is evident that to anyone who had the power of moving freely in four dimensions it would be possible to move up the mass and see what some cross section was like which had not yet arrived at our space.

This is desperately crude but it gives the general idea.

In order to grasp it better we will transpose it into terms of two-and three space at the same time altering it slightly. Suppose that a two space world consists of a colossal soap film. Imagine a thin thread passing through the film and stretched between two points, one above the film and one below.

If these two points move perpendicularly to the film the thread will move accordingly. The point where the thread cuts the film will remain stationary if the thread was perpendicular to the latter to start with, but will move if the thread was originally slanting.

To a two space being inhabiting the film, all that will be visible of the thread will be a minute circle, an atom of two-space matter let us say.

Now let us imagine an enormous number of such threads, sufficient to produce all the atoms necessary to make up a complete two space universe. Suppose also that these are twisted and intertwined in the most complicated possible manner. Then as they pass across the soap film they will give rise to the most complex changes in the two space world.

A three space being, however, could see the filamentary structure as a whole and would not be limited to the particular section which happened to be crossing the film at any given moment.

I must again insist that I do not for a moment regard this as being anything like a true picture of what actually occurs. The point I wish to make is merely that if, as seems to be the case, three space change can be represented spatially by the use of four space ideas, then it is not utterly inconceivable that a consciousness free to move in four space and independent of three space limitations, should be able in some obscure way to foresee coming changes.

There is a prevalent notion to the effect that if we admit the possibility of prevision we are bound to become involved in the slough of Fatalism.

"If we can foresee what is going to happen," it is urged, "then the future must be already settled, and we have no power of altering it."

This view appears to me to be fallacious.

Consider again for a moment the filamentary world.

Our forecast of events therein is based on the assumption that the filamentary structures remain unaltered, that the cross-sections which will be traversed by the film will not be changed before it gets there.

This is pure assumption and quite unwarranted.

In the first place the two space beings themselves might be able to alter the arrangement of the threads during their passage across the film, implying of course the exercise of three space forces, and the possession of a certain degree of three-dimensionality, on their part. In the second place all sorts of extraneous three space forces might be applied.

The argument does not perhaps apply especially felicitously to this particular analogy, but translated into more general terms it means that three space change, although expressible in terms of four space, and perhaps for the very reason that it is thus expressible, is susceptible to modification under the influence of factors which have no three-dimensionality.

As stated at the outset, absolute prevision necessitates *every* factor being accounted for, and these factors may appear, not merely in three space or four space, but in N-space too.

In fact, the more accurate prevision is to be, the wider survey must the percipient take.

In order to attain absolute prevision the precipient must be able to function consciously in maximally-dimensional space. But this ability I take to be the exclusive prerogative of the Divine Consciousness.

The purely speculatory character of the foregoing will be evident and I do not wish it to be taken as more than an attempt to convey a general impression of ideas which seem somewhat suggestive.

It seems appropriate to end a chapter frankly given over to inchoate and somewhat formless speculations, with some remarks on the objectivity or otherwise of space in general.

These remarks have been more especially prompted by Mr. E.L. Gardner's article on "The Fourth Dimension" which appeared in the *Theosophist* for October 1916, by a pamphlet for private circulation written by Mr. T. Olman Todd, 1915, and by Mr. Klein's remarks on Space in his book "Science and the Infinite."

Throughout this work I have treated four-dimensional space as an objective reality and, as will appear, I consider that this is perfectly justifiable.

The general tendency of the above-mentioned writers seems to be to suggest that this attitude is fallacious and that all space, of whatever dimensionality, is rather to be regarded as a phenomenon of consciousness. In saying this I do not pretend to be reflecting with precision the views expressed by the writers in question. I am merely giving the general effect produced on my mind by their ideas.

I may say at once that I think that they are probably perfectly right and that no space of any kind is really objective.

I am, for instance, disposed to agree with Mr. Gardner when he says that "However willingly we may grant that behind the description 'Fourth

Dimension' there stands something that is real, it is of importance that that reality should be described in terms of Life and Consciousness and not be regarded as a further extension of Matter or Form."

Mr. Klein concludes that "our very conception of space is one of the modes only under which motion or physical phenomena are presented to our consciousness."

I have neither the knowledge nor the temerity to embark upon a discussion of the point from the metaphysical point of view and all I wish to do is to show that I am aware that all our ideas regarding space are liable to be modified at the hands of the philosophers and that I have no desire to minimise the importance of their contributions. On the contrary I think it probable that these may prove to be of the utmost value. They may, for instance, by interpreting spatial experience in terms of consciousness, throw light on the very considerable difficulty to which I drew attention on page 48.

But I submit that for the present purpose we can legitimately disregard the whole thing. It may well be that the change in passing from our present state of consciousness to that which I have described as consciousness in four dimensions is subjective rather than objective, that the change would be in our consciousness rather than in spatial conditions. But whatever may be the real nature of our three-dimensional space from the strictly academic point of view we can and habitually do treat it as an objective reality and I think it fair to claim an equal licence in dealing with four-dimensional space.

Pure consciousness is an elusive thing to handle and if we find evidence to the effect, for example, that the state of consciousness in which we exist when separated from the body can be accurately represented by the higher space hypothesis, then surely we had better say that it is existence in four-dimensional space and have done with it, just as we say that our normal existence is existence in three dimensional space.

After all the whole matter is one of "relativity" so to speak. The final effect with which we are concerned is the reaction of reality on our minds and, just as we can in dynamics reduce any one member of a system to rest and treat all motions as relative to that so here it makes no practical difference whether it is our mind or reality which changes provided that the changed relation between them is correctly expressed.

CHAPTER V

VITALITY AND WILL

Another and particularly happy illustration of the way in which the higher space concepts enable one to solve awkward dilemmas is to be found in the problems of Vitality and Will. Readers who are interested in these topics would do well to refer to Mr. Hereward Carrington's "Problems of Psychical Research" or to his "Vitality, Fasting, and Nutrition."

There are in general two main views which may be taken about Vitality. We may either suppose that Life is purely a product of the body, that it is a mere physiological function and nothing more, or one may suppose that so far from the body being the primary cause of Life the exact converse is the case—that Life is the *raison d'etre* of the body. It may be that everything that we recognize as "vital," every attribute which enables us to distinguish animate from inanimate objects, is no more than a purely physical phenomenon the product of unusually complicated chemical actions: or it may be that the chemico-physical complex which we call the body is only the means whereby the pressing tide of Life manages to manifest itself in the world. This latter is the view held by M. Bergson, by Mr. Carrington and by myself.

"M. Bergson regards matter as the dam which keeps back the rush of life. Organise it a little (as in the protozoa), *i.e.*, slightly raise the sluice,—and a little life will squeeze through. Organise it elaborately (as in man), *i.e.*, raise the sluice a good deal, and much life will squeeze through."

(The Right Hon. A.J. Balfour.)

This is the "transmissive" as opposed to the "productive" theory and the whole position is very like that which obtained in Psychology some years ago. William James then showed that although it was possible to interpret the observed facts of Psychology on the hypothesis that the brain "produced" consciousness it was equally legitimate to do so on the hypothesis that it "transmitted" it.

As he said " ... Mere coincidence in two sets of phenomena does not prove that they are causally connected, that one produces the other. They may be quite separate from one another (psycho-physical parallelism) or both may be aspects of something else."

Personally I should be prepared to admit only the latter possibility. Causeless parallelism is incredible; as James himself admits elsewhere.

The analogy is very close. Just as consciousness is usually conceived to be due to the functioning of the brain but may, on the contrary exist apart from it and merely use the brain as a channel of manifestation, so also may Life exist apart from and use the body.

I will not go into the various arguments which support this view. Perhaps the most striking is that from the necessity for sleep—a phenomenon which appears to be exclusively associated with Life. A mechanism needs replenishing with fuel, it must have worn parts replaced and both these processes are accurately paralleled in the body of any living organism. But an engine does not need sleep, whereas a living organism not only needs it but cannot be satisfied with any substitute for it. It looks therefore as if Life could not be maintained from purely physical sources and this lends support to the view that it is an essentially extra-physical thing transmitted by, but not arising from, physical actions.

But this view leaves us with the difficulty that if we suppose that Life is transcendent to the Physical and uses it only as a means of manifestation we cannot see how it can do so without partaking of the nature of the physical and so losing its "selective," "guiding" or "intelligent" qualities. For in order that things should be causally connected they must have qualities in common. Are then we to say that life is a form of energy or that it is not?

As Mr. Carrington says: "We are ... driven into this dilemma: life must be an energy—but, as such, it cannot be purposive! Life is purposive, yet it must be an energy—for otherwise it could not affect the bodily energies and the material world."

M. Bergson adopts the "hair trigger" theory and supposes the Life only affects the physical energies of the body *very slightly*, just enough to deflect them this way or that. But this is not getting out of the difficulty at all, for the problem is one not of degree but of kind; it is just as difficult to imagine "non-energy" affecting energy "very slightly" as to imagine it affecting it a good deal.

Nor does it help matters to suppose, with Mr. Carrington and other authorities, that Life is a wholly distinct and unique kind of energy; an "absolutely separate force *per se* different from any other mode of energy of which we have any knowledge." If this is so we must ask "How is it that this force combines sufficient of the qualities common to all the physical forces to enable it to affect them, with characteristics of so different a nature that we can call it an absolutely different force *per se* and emancipate it from the ordinary laws and limitations of physical forces?"

A very similar, if not identical, dilemma arises in the case of Will which must either be supposed to be a purely physical force—which hypothesis commits us at once to a creed of thoroughgoing materialistic determinism or else we must suppose it to be distinct from physical energy by virtue of some added non-physical quality which must be wholly outside the physical realm. Yet this extra quality of "conscious intent" which is the essential characteristic of the act of willing does, as a matter of common experience, enable us to control physical matter and forces.

In fact, the whole trouble is simply this.

The universe presents a closed circle of matter and energy. Anything within it must be bound by law, blind and unintelligent. Nothing without it can affect anything within it—if for no other reason than that if it could it would violate the fundamental law of the conservation of energy. But Will *does* affect matter, therefore it must be within the circle: it is *not* blind, for its very essence is initiative, independence, and intelligence and it must, therefore, be outside the circle.

Now let us introduce the idea of higher space and see where it leads us.

Suppose that the energy which we term "Life" is located to start with in higher space—in four-dimensional space for example. Suppose that it is really pressing against the "dam" of three-dimensional matter trying to use it for a vehicle of manifestation. The extent to which it will be able to do so will depend on the presence or absence in the matter concerned of those qualities which enable it to be acted on by four-dimensional forces. What these qualities are it is at present impossible to say although one might hazard a guess to the effect that the essential factor might be one of greater or less molecular extension in the direction of the fourth dimension.

But wherever matter exists which possesses the suitable properties, there will Life "squeeze through the dam" to a greater or less extent and we shall have a "living" organism which will continue to live until the matter through which Life is—in each particular case—manifesting, loses the properties which enable it to be made use of.

Whether there is any sort of matter which can truly be called completely inanimate or whether, as some people hold, all matter is to some extent "alive" I am not prepared to say. Personally I should be sorry to have to draw a distinct dividing line anywhere and it seems more in accordance with the general continuity of things to suppose that no such line can really be drawn.

For myself I tend more and more to the view that Life, Vitality, Consciousness—call it what you will—is something which dips down, as it were, for the purpose of gaining experience and of self-evolution, from its original location—wherever and whatever that may be—through successive limitations of consciousness until it reaches this, the lowest, the most restricted and the most individual state of all.

These successive limitations may conveniently be represented by saying that consciousness functions in spaces of successively decreasing dimensionality although it must be borne in mind, as was pointed out at the end of the last chapter, that this may be only a convenient way of expressing the effect of a change which belongs to the consciousness itself more properly than to its environment.

At each successive descent consciousness must find a suitably organised vehicle in which to function and through which it can receive impressions. But each such vehicle will involve corresponding circumscriptions and, conversely, each upward stage will involve an extension of consciousness, until finally, when our evolution is entirely accomplished, we shall be completely and fully Conscious and independent of all limitations of any sort or kind. On the downward half of the journey the characteristic process would, on this theory, be the gaining of individual at the cost of "communal" consciousness, whereas during the second half the latter would continually increase and at last lead to complete "communion" in the widest possible sense without any loss of individuality. This view, which has a good deal to support it especially in point of continuity and general coherence with other well established ideas, has much in common with that held by the Theosophists, which is, to my mind, the strongest plank in their platform.

But to revert to the original idea of Life as primarily a four-dimensional force.

This does not involve any contravention of the Law of the Conservation of energy for we have only to suppose that the Law is exact only for the Cosmos and for the physical universe, as commonly understood, no more than a very close approximation.

The amounts of energy which we must suppose to enter the physical or three-dimensional universe from four-dimensional space may be very small, so small as to defy detection by the methods we are able to apply to the study of living organisms in which alone they could be observed; and yet, by virtue of the "hair-trigger" theory to which I have already referred they might produce effects as large as we please.

The foregoing is clearly incomplete, but I think I may fairly claim to have removed the fundamental dilemma which first confronted us.

We have seen that life may be supposed to exist entirely apart from ordinary physical matter and yet to affect it so long as we suppose it to do so from some region of higher space. It is a form of energy if we wish to call it so and yet it is distinct from the ordinary forms of physical energy and free from the limitations which would be imposed upon it if we reckoned it as subject to the Law of Conservation as commonly understood.

And yet the latter is not broken but rather strengthened; for we now suppose it to be not merely of Universal but of Cosmic application.

CHAPTER VI

HIGHER SPACE AND PHYSICAL SCIENCE.

In an earlier chapter I defined a valid hypothesis as one which explained at least *some* of the observed facts and did not contradict any of them.

Since then I have been trying to show that the Higher Space ideas do throw a certain amount of light on quite a number of difficulties and enable us to clear up certain anomalies and dilemmas which seem to be insoluble without its aid.

We must now consider rather more definitely than we have hitherto done whether there is any thing in the hypothesis to conflict with those established conclusions of scientists which are the nearest approach we have to absolute certainties. I think we shall find not only that there is no such conflict but that there are here and there distinct indications that the higher space ideas may some day find applications in the exegesis of even the most strictly physical sciences.

These indications are admittedly very nebulous at present, it may be that they are all illusory and as will appear later they cannot *all* lead to anything, for some are mutually exclusive.

I do not propose to express any very definite opinions on their comparative values but shall simply state them and leave it to my readers to decide what they are worth.

It must be remembered throughout that we cannot expect to find any very definite indications of the existence of higher space as a reality for the simple reason that physical science is concerned solely with those phenomena of matter and force which are "*ex hypothesi*" essentially three-dimensional.

It is worth noting at the outset that physical scientists have evinced no especial hostility to the concept of the fourth dimension, as such, however much they may have opposed to the more definitely Psychic researches which I, personally, believe to be closely associated with it.

Lord Kelvin, for instance, saw in it nothing repugnant to scientific thought and professed himself quite willing to adopt it should such a course seem to be indicated by the evidence. Another distinguished physicist has gone so far as to evolve a theory of "ether squirts" from the direction of the fourth dimension in connection with the ultimate constitution of matter.

Again M. Poincaré the distinguished French Physicist has said "The characteristic property of space, that of having three dimensions is only ... a property residing, so to speak, in human intelligence."

Mathematical physicists also find that certain experimental anomalies are resolved if they refer phenomena to four interchangeable axes involving homogeneous co-ordinates instead of to three space axes and one time axis. If this is not dealing in four-dimensional space it is first cousin to it.

M. Poincaré also pointed out that the postulates of Euclid are not experimentally verifiable facts and as a matter of fact much work has been done in the elaboration of non-Euclidean geometries. This is too mathematical a subject to be dealt with in detail here, but I can indicate the general drift of it, so far as it is relevant to the present discussion by means of the time honoured analogy of the two-dimensional world.

Most of my readers will know what are meant by the terms "latitude" and "longitude" and that the lines of longitude are "great circles" which pass through the poles and cut the earth's equator at right angles. It is also a matter of common knowledge that if on a plane surface two lines are drawn each of which cuts another line at right angles these two lines will be parallel—that is to say they will never meet however far they may be produced. This holds good provided that the surface in which they are drawn is truly plane—*i.e.,* flat. But it breaks down, as we see in the case of the "great circles" of longitude, if the lines are drawn on a sphere. Now imagine two-dimensional beings, having no conception of the existence of a third dimension, living on the surface of a very large sphere. They might discover this principle about parallel lines and all would go well until they began making measurements over very large distances. Then their Geometry would begin to go wrong. They would find that lines drawn in their surface which ought not to meet however far produced would begin to show a tendency to do so. This would be an indication to them that there was such a thing as a third dimension of space and that their two-dimensional world was curved in this third dimension.

Now if a two-dimensional space can be curved in three dimensions there is no sort of reason why three-dimensional space should not be curved in four and in a precisely similar way three-dimensional geometry would, if such were the case, begin to "go wrong" where very large measurements were involved. Now, the largest measurements we ever make are astronomical measurements and as a matter of fact, according to Mr. Bragdon, there does seem to be a tendency for Geometry to go wrong in certain cases. He says that the number of negative parallaxes of stars is larger than would be expected having regard to the probable experimental errors. The parallax of an object is the angle which it subtends at two different points of observation, and so long as it is at a finite distance from these two points—which in the case of a star are the two opposite ends of the earth's orbit—this angle must be positive. That is to say the lines drawn in the observed direction of the star from the two points must converge.

If, as in certain cases seems to happen, they *diverge*, then one of three things must be the case; either the observations are wrong or else light does not, as is commonly believed, travel in straight lines (for after all what we call a straight line in astronomy is only the path of a ray of light) or else our geometry is breaking down and we must suppose that our space is curved, which would necessitate the acceptance of the existence of a fourth dimension.

It must be admitted that the explanation of negative parallaxes is more likely to be found in one or both of the two first alternatives than in the third.

Mr. Hinton has a good deal to say in his books about various four-dimensional theories of electricity involving four-dimensional vortices. These are highly ingenious but there does not seem to be any considerable reason for supposing them to be anything more and I shall therefore not describe them here. Two of his ideas however are so striking, although for different reasons, that I think a brief outline will not be out of place.

In his book "A new Era of Thought" he points out the remarkable analogy which exists between the properties of ether as postulated by physicists and those which a perfectly smooth solid sheet would present to the intelligence of two-dimensional beings living on it.

The hypothesis of the ether was introduced to account for the transmission of light, heat, electricity, and so forth, and has proved of the utmost service to physicists. Most of my readers are probably acquainted with the general idea and I need not therefore discuss it in detail.

It will be sufficient here to say that it is supposed to be a weightless, homogeneous medium extending throughout all space and permeating all bodies. Indeed Matter itself is supposed to be no more than the result of more or less complex disturbances in it.

But although it accounts for the phenomena in connection with which it was called into being it is necessary to ascribe to it very contradictory properties. On the one hand it has been calculated that in order for it to transmit the forces which we know that it does transmit, for instance the force of gravitation, it must possess a rigidity some 3,000 times greater than that of the strongest known steel. On the other hand we must suppose it to be of a tenuity far in excess of the most perfect vacuum which we can obtain, for otherwise the earth and other planets which are moving at immense speed through this medium would be slowed down; which is not in practice the case.

Now Hinton points out that to a two-dimensional being, a perfectly smooth solid sheet on the surface of which he lived would possess many of these properties. Being perfectly smooth it would be imperceptible to him and would offer no opposition to the passage of bodies over it. Yet it could, being solid, transmit vibration just as we know the ether does for us. Also it could be as rigid as you please without losing any of its imperceptibility. It could not be weighed and it could not be eliminated from any vessel no matter what care was taken to do so.

The analogy is striking but it does not appeal to me and I do not think that even Mr. Hinton means it to be taken strictly, for in other passages he gives quite different suggestions as to the ether.

One of the latter is derived from a consideration of the phenomena of rotation in four-dimensional space and is of some intrinsic interest.

In two space rotation takes place about a point, in three space about a line and we should therefore expect that in four space it would do so about a plane. This is easily shown to be the case although I do not propose to go into the proof here. The only important point is that whereas it is impossible to conceive a mass of three-dimensional spheres in a state of continuous rotation,—because they would be trying to drive each other in different directions and so would prevent the rotation,—in four dimensions this is not the case and a mass of "hyper-spheres" could be "self-driving," that is to say the rotation of each could be such as to assist and not to retard that of its neighbours. This fact is of interest because Lord Kelvin showed that the contradictory properties of the ether referred to above could only be reconciled by supposing it to be animated throughout by a motion of a vortical character.

This "self-driving" effect of rotating hyper-spheres is worth glancing at a little more closely. It arises from the fact that there are two distinct sorts of rotation which such a sphere may possess. In three-dimensional rotation the motion may take place about any axis we please and the other two axes which can be drawn will change one into the other, so to speak, as the rotation takes place. But in four-dimensional space we have four axes and while the X and Y axes change place, say, there is nothing to prevent the W and Z axes doing so too. Thus we might have the X axis changing into the Y and the W into the Z. To reverse both of these motions so as to have the Y axis changing into the X and the Z into the W does not give us a new kind of motion any more than reversing the direction of an ordinary three-dimensional rotation does—it is only equivalent to looking at it from a different point of view. But if in the case of the four-dimensional rotation we reverse one only of the two rotational components we do get a new kind of motion, and this is of interest in view of the fact that electricity like other forces is regarded as a mode of etheric motion, and if this be so there would seem to be a certain need for two distinct kinds of it in order to correspond to positive and negative electricity respectively.

It is just possible that there is some connection, as Mr. Hinton suggests, between this need and the two kinds of four-dimensional rotation referred to above.

Most writers on the subject of higher space make great play with the phenomena of symmetry and adduce its occurrence in nature as evidence of the existence of a fourth dimension. This view is not warranted by the facts and I shall therefore touch on it only very briefly.

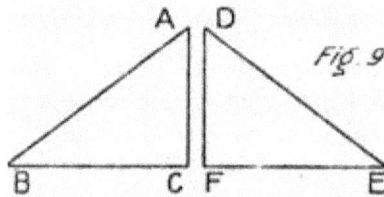

Fig. 9

The point arises in the following way. Consider the two triangles ABC and DEF in Fig. 9. If these were cut out and laid on a smooth surface exactly as shown, no amount of sliding about would enable us to fit one exactly over the other. In order to do this it would be necessary to pick one up out of the plane of the paper and turn it over. In a precisely similar manner two asymmetrical three-dimensional objects such as a right and left hand, each of which is the mirror image of the other, could not be made to coincide unless one of them were to be turned over in four-dimensional space. The point made by Mr. Hinton and other writers who attach importance to the phenomena of symmetry, is that there seems to be a general tendency in nature towards a right and left handed symmetry in which the whole organism is symmetrical about a central plane, each half being the mirror image of the other and that this symmetry is unlikely to have arisen through equal increments on either side of the central plane. They suppose as an alternative that "the ultimate elements of living matter" are not right and left handed *ab initio*, but become so by virtue of some of them being "folded over" in four-dimensional space.

This view seems to me to lack foundation especially in view of the fact that the work of Le Bel and Van't Hoff fully cleared up the analogous phenomena in the case of crystals without introducing the concept of higher space at all. In general therefore I agree with Schubert who says:—

" ... the only inference we can here make is that the idea of a four-dimensioned space is competent, from a mathematical point of view, to throw some light on the phenomena of symmetry."

(Mathematical Essays, p. 91.)

None the less Bragdon is right in his contention that "Could it be shown that the two-dimensional symmetry in nature is the result of a three dimensional movement, the right and left-handed symmetry of solids would by analogy be the result of a four-dimensional movement."

I need hardly say that if we could experimentally obtain the changing of an asymmetrical right-handed object into the corresponding left-handed one it would be of the very first importance as a proof of the reality of higher space.

Far more important than any of the foregoing, however, are the considerations arising from what is known as the Principle of Relativity. This subject, which has received much attention at the hands of mathematical physicists in recent years, is far too abstruse to be dealt with in detail here and a partial and popularised account would almost certainly fail to satisfy those who are not wholly ignorant of mathematical physics and would weary those who are. I propose, therefore, to dismiss it in very few words in spite of its great importance and relevance.

"The Principle of Relativity is the hypothesis that it is impossible by means of physical experiments to determine the absolute velocity of a body through space." (Cunningham "Relativity and the Electron Theory," p. 2).

We cannot, for example, determine the velocity of the earth relative to the ether.

This is of importance when we are dealing with the idea of "simultaneity"— an idea which, as we saw in Chapter IV. is closely associated with our notion of Time. For our criterion of simultaneity has in practice been based on optical communication. (Cp. Ibid, pp. 5 and 28). But it is easy to show that "the setting up of a standard of simultaneity by means of light signals is not possible until a definite velocity is assigned to the observer. Thus the hypothesis of relativity requires a reconsideration of the way in which we measure time." (Ibid, pp. 5, 28, 29).

"This again reacts on the measurement of the length of a material body, the 'distance between two points' being the distance between simultaneous positions of those points. Thus it becomes necessary also to examine the way in which we measure space. It becomes impossible to consider space and time separately; the two measures are interrelated to such an extent that Minkowski felt himself constrained to say that 'from henceforth time by itself and space by itself are mere shadows, that they are only two aspects of a single and indivisible manner of co-ordinating the facts of the physical world.'" (Ibid, pp. 5 and 6.)

When it is remembered that the Principle of Relativity is firmly established in scientific thought it will be realised that this conclusion arrived at as a result of purely physical considerations is of the very utmost importance as an independent confirmation of the general line of thought developed in the preceding pages.

I therefore feel it legitimate to claim that in so far as physical science throws any light on the subject at all its testimony is distinctly favourable.

CHAPTER VII

THE CONNECTING LINK

In the foregoing chapters I have tried to show that there are, scattered here and there over the field of Psychic Research, sufficient indications to warrant our adopting, as a tentative working hypothesis, the idea that four-dimensional space is a reality and that the Individual consciousness is capable of functioning in a four-dimensional vehicle quite apart from the three-dimensional physical body.

I hope that I have made it quite clear that in my opinion the two vehicles are entirely separate and independent, and that I do not regard the three-dimensional body as being a mere section of a four-dimensional whole.

I propose in this chapter to consider in some detail the question of the nature of the connection which must perforce exist between the two vehicles.

We know that there must be some form of connection because impressions which are received by the three-dimensional sense organs are transmitted to the conscious Ego, which is, *ex hypothesi*, embodied in the four-dimensional vehicle.

Furthermore it is clear that the connection can be interrupted with comparative ease, since in sleep, anæsthesia, and analogous conditions, the conscious Ego does not receive these impressions although the sense organs may still be subject to stimuli to a greater or less degree.

We are not, of course, able to draw detailed conclusions as to the precise nature of this connection by the exercise of pure deductive reason.

But I think that my readers will agree with me that the first and most obvious place to look for it will be in the realm of the nervous system.

Further we may safely say that, assuming the hypothesis we are considering to be correct, the sense impression must, at some stage in its transmission, be deflected, so to speak, out of three space into four space.

In order for this to happen it is necessary that some part of the transmitting mechanism should be capable of producing this deflection and it is reasonable to suppose that a substance or mechanism specially differentiated for the purpose of deflecting impressions in this manner out of three space into four space, will be distinguished by an abnormal four-dimensional complexity as compared with ordinary matter, which, as we have already seen, probably possesses a very slight four-dimensional extension.

As a result of this abnormal four-dimensional complexity it is to be anticipated that the part of the transmitting mechanism concerned will possess characteristics sufficient to differentiate it from ordinary matter.

I submit, then, that we may reasonably deduce that if the four-dimensional hypothesis which I have outlined be correct, there should exist, either as an integral part of the nervous system or in close association with it, some constituent or substance which, in spite of having many of the properties of ordinary matter, will also possess characteristics peculiar to itself—as, for instance, susceptibility to four-dimensional forces imperceptible to us.

At this point I would recall to the reader's attention the remarks which I made in Chapter II regarding the processes of scientific thought and the sequence of operations whereby we attain to exact knowledge.

So far we have considered a number of observed facts and framed a working hypothesis which, I believe, explains some, and is not contradicted by any, of them.

In the immediately preceding paragraphs we have, by deductive reasoning, concluded that if this hypothesis be correct then something else must follow. There must, in fact, be some sort of connecting link whereby sense impressions are deflected out of three space into four space and are thus enabled to get through to the consciousness.

We have also concluded that this connecting link is likely to consist of matter in some curious condition such as to invest it with properties unlike those of ordinary matter. If on turning again to the realm of observation, we find that this deduction is substantiated in practice, we shall receive distinct confirmation of the correctness of our working hypothesis.

In the pages which follow I propose to show that there are a number of facts which strongly indicate, even if they cannot at present be held conclusively to demonstrate, the existence of some such connecting link.

I am well aware that there are numerous gaps in the body of evidence which I shall bring forward on this subject. To some of these I shall draw specific attention in the hope that by doing so I may induce some of my readers to experiment on the points in question. There is an enormous amount of research work to be done before we shall be able to have any considerable confidence in our speculations or to feel that we are working on anything like a firm foundation. Much of the evidence to which I shall refer in this chapter is in urgent need of confirmation and there is very little indeed which I should care to guarantee personally. Still the indications, slight though they are, do seem to point rather in the same direction and as my object is to stimulate investigation and, perhaps to indicate some of the lines on which it may profitably proceed rather than to lay down the law on obscure points, I have thought it worth while to deal with them fairly fully.

Historically the first relevant experiments were probably those of Reichenbach in the middle of last century. But so little was known in those days about a variety of factors which might have vitiated his results, and his work has been so strongly criticised by later authorities that I will not do more than mention him for the benefit of any reader who may have a fancy for probing into the historical origins of the subject. None the less great credit is due to Reichenbach for the thorough and painstaking character of his researches to which he brought immense industry and a truly scientific spirit which led him to fantastic and erroneous conclusions only because he had not our present knowledge to guard him from the many pitfalls which abound in these investigations.

The first phenomena to which I wish to call attention is that known as Exteriorisation of Sensibility.

This has been investigated by de Rochas and later by Joire and by Boirac, and I believe it is well established.

The gist of the phenomenon is that in certain hypnotic states the skin of the subject becomes insensitive to pain but the "sensibility" is transferred to a sensitive layer a few centimetres distant from the skin. Pinching or pricking the skin itself produces no effect but doing so in the region of the sensitive layer arouses the appropriate sensation in the subject. Furthermore, according to Joire, this sensibility can be localised and transferred to various objects—a fact which gives the investigator a most desirable power of experimental control.

Dr. Joire performed a number of experiments to determine whether the results could be attributed to auto-suggestion, to unconscious suggestion by the investigator or to unconscious connivance on the part of the subject, but concluded that they could not. Any reader who has doubts on the subject should read his book "Psychical and Supernormal Phenomena." Dr. Joire was unable to give any explanation of these phenomena, nor shall I attempt to do so at the moment beyond pointing out that on the face of it, it looks as if some definite substance of sensitive properties were exteriorised which, however, must be supposed to be to some extent under the control of the will, since it was found that the seat of sensibility could be shifted at the word of command.

Leaving this for a moment I would draw attention to the subject of the "aura." Certain persons claim to be able to see this normally as a regular thing and describe it as being a bluish-grey haze surrounding the body and at a little distance from it. Dr. Kilner in his book "The Human Atmosphere" describes how he found it possible to induce this power of vision in normal persons by causing them to gaze at the light through suitably coloured screens which seemed to affect the retina in such a way as to make it more sensitive to the particular wave length of light which emanates from, or is reflected by, the aura.

In the course of his investigations he found among other things that the aura was apparently under the control of the will since it could in certain cases be made to change colour or to extrude rays by mere volition.

Through the courtesy of Dr. Kilner I have myself been able to try the effect of the screens and I certainly saw, or thought I saw, an aura of the type which he describes.

At the same time I am not altogether prepared to swear that the appearance could not be some sort of optical illusion or "artifact" and I should accept the aura with less reserve if it could be recorded photographically.

On the other hand some of Dr. Kilner's experiments, notably as regards colour of the aura and its uses in diagnosis, are very remarkable and seem unlikely to be due to either of the above mentioned causes.

If we accept these experiments at their face value they certainly support the idea to which the phenomena of Exteriorisation of Sensibility faintly pointed, namely that there may be some exteriorisable *substance* under the control of the Will.

There are other experiments which also point the same way. Consider for example those of MacDougal who weighed a number of patients at the moment of death and found in each case that this coincided with a *sudden* loss of weight of about threequarters of an ounce, more than could be accounted for by loss from perspiration or from the emptying of the lungs. He claims that "We have experimental proof that a substance capable of being weighed does leave the body at death." It is of course most important that these experiments should be confirmed by independent investigators but there seems no reason to doubt the facts as stated, although I cannot agree with MacDougal's view that what leaves the body *is* the "soul."

Dr. Baraduc, again, took photographs of his son and wife shortly after death and found that in each case a luminous, cloudlike mass or masses were visible over the bodies.

This case is of exceptional interest in that the observations were not personal but were photographic records. Unless the case is inaccurately reported it follows that there must have been some objective foundation for the results, and it would also seem that, since the object photographed affected the plate but was invisible to the eye, it must not only have been material or quasi-material in nature but also have emitted light of a frequency above the range of normal vision, *i.e.*, "ultra-violet" light. Here again there is great need for confirmation but so far as it goes the evidence continues to point the same way.

Surely this concatenation of evidences from such different sources cannot be purely fortuitous?

The foregoing are the most important and representative experiments on these lines but the whole of the literature of Psychic Research abounds with minor pointers which all indicate the same sort of thing.

Let us turn again to the work of Crawford, to which I have already referred.

He started out to investigate the causes of telekinetic phenomena and had at the outset no sort of notion of what the explanation was likely to be and he found that his table is supported, during levitation without contact, by a rigid structure.

This structure is invisible to the eye and is practically impalpable. It appears to be composed of matter taken from the medium. The main conclusion is, I think, inevitable, but for the experiments and reasoning which have led to it the reader must consult Dr. Crawford's book.

Again we have this same curious substance exteriorised from the body.

But there are two points in particular which bring it closely into line with the phenomena which we have been considering.

The first is that although Dr. Crawford has not yet succeeded in photographing the structure *in situ*, he has obtained a photograph of what appears to be the same substance issuing out of the medium.

Furthermore, the existence of the structure has been confirmed by clairvoyants, and this fact, taken in conjunction with the photographic results and with what I said about "etheric" or "ultra-violet" clairvoyance in Chapter III, forces us once more to the conclusion that this elusive substance possesses the property of emitting or reflecting ultra-violet light.

The second point is that the extrusion of this substance from the medium results in superficial insensibility, although she is in full possession of all her normal faculties.

Dr. Crawford discusses this point at some length in an article which appeared in the *Psychic Gazette* for September 1916. Into the minutiæ of the discussion

I need not enter here. It is sufficient to say that the medium is to some extent insensitive and that in Dr. Crawford's opinion "It seems likely that the want of sensibility to heavy and varied reactions which undoubtedly occur upon the medium is due to some peculiar condition of her organism during the period of phenomena."

Now, these various experiments although they may be individually weak do seem rather to hang together. There is an appearance of possible connection between the experiments of Joire and recent views on the "aura"; and it is possible that what MacDougal weighed and Baraduc photographed are the same thing.

It is obvious that all these experiments ought to be checked and re-checked by independent investigators and further experiments undertaken to discover whether there is any real connection between them.

But for the present purpose I think it legitimate to extrapolate and to assume that they are reliable and connected in the way that I suspect.

The experiments of de Rochas, of Joire and of Kilner suggest that a temporary loss of sensibility is accompanied by the extrusion from the body of a sensitive substance of peculiar properties.

In the Baraduc and MacDougal experiments a total and permanent loss of sensibility seems to be accompanied by the extrusion of a substance of somewhat similar properties.

Finally in the case of Dr. Crawford's researches we find that the extrusion of an apparently very similar substance is again accompanied by a certain insensitivity.

Somewhat similar conditions are to be found in cases of "materialisation"—compare, for example, the work of Dr. Schrenk-Notzing and Mme. Bisson or Dr. Geley's paper in Part I. of the "Annales des Sciences Psychiques" for 1919.

It is far too early yet to say that the extrusion of this sensitive substance is an invariable concomitant of insensibility; but at present the evidence—assuming it to be reliable—does seem to point that way. When we have made an exhaustive study of what happens to the "aura" during sleep, in various states of hypnosis, in local and general anæsthesia and in death we shall be able to draw more definite conclusions on the subject.

I shall now turn to evidence of a more general type which deals with the existence of this mysterious substance viewed as a whole rather than with this or that indication of its presence or properties as did the previous experiments.

There are many references in Psychic literature which bear on the point and the general trend of them seems to be that the substance we have been considering is not, normally, entirely formless and distributed fortuitously through the body but that it forms an exact counterpart of the latter or, to be more strictly accurate, of the nervous system.

Lombroso states that Durville has succeeded in separating this "replica" experimentally from the physical body.

("After Death—What?").

He says that it seemed to be connected with the body by a sort of cord and that the patient under observation was able to see through opaque objects and to discern events at a distance. The apparent sense organs of the replica worked, while those of the physical body were put out of action. When approached, it excited a sensation "like that produced by cold, by blowing air, by shivering," and if the hand were placed in it a cold, clammy sensation was experienced. Compare with this last statement the remarks of Crawford on the sensations produced by inserting the hand into the midst of the levitating structure.

M. Leon Denis in "Christianity and Spiritualism" quotes experiments from the "Revue Spirite" for November 1894, and alleges that de Rochas and Barlemont obtained simultaneous photographs of the body of a medium and of the exteriorised "double."

A long account of experiments on these lines by Durville appears in the "Journal de Magnetisme" for 1907 and 1908 but although they tend to confirm the ideas at which we have already arrived, there is nothing to be gained by going into their details here.

A very interesting case which has a considerable bearing on the subject is given in the Proceedings of the Society for Psychical Research, Vol. VIII, pp. 180-193.

The following is an abbreviated account:

The narrator is a physician and the case seems to have been singularly well attested and was carefully scrutinised by no less a critic than Dr. R.H. Hodgson.

"I passed some four hours in all without pulse or perceptible heart beat, as I am informed by Dr. S.H. Raynes, who was the only physician present. During a portion of this time several of the bystanders thought I was dead, and, such a report being carried outside, the village church bell was tolled. Dr. Raynes informs me, however, that by bringing his eyes close to my face, he could perceive an occasional short gasp, so very light as to be hardly perceptible, and that he was several times on the point of saying, 'He is dead,' when a gasp would occur in time to check him. He thrust a needle deep into the flesh at different points from the feet to the hips, but got no response.[5] Although I was pulseless for four hours, the state of apparent death lasted only about half an hour. I lost, I believe, all power of thought or knowledge of existence in absolute unconsciousness. I came again into a state of conscious existence, and discovered that I was still in the body, but the body and I had no longer any interests in common. I looked with astonishment and joy for the first time upon myself—the *me*, the real Ego, while the not-me closed upon all sides like a sepulchre of clay. With all the interest of a physician I beheld the wonders of my bodily anatomy, intimately interwoven with which, even tissue for tissue, was I, the living soul of that dead body. I realised my condition and calmly reasoned thus: I have died, as man terms death, and yet I am as much a man as ever. I am about to get out of the body. I watched the interesting process of the separation of soul and body. By some power, apparently not my own, the Ego was rocked to and fro, laterally as the cradle is rocked, by which process its connection with the tissues of the body was broken up. After a little while the lateral motions ceased, and along the soles of the feet, beginning at the toes, passing rapidly to the heels, I felt and heard, as it seemed the snapping of innumerable small cords. When this was accomplished, I began slowly to retreat from the feet, toward the head, as a rubber cord shortens. I remember reaching the hips and saying to myself, 'Now there is no life below the hips.' I can recall no memory of passing through the abdomen and chest, but recollect distinctly when my whole self was collected in the head, when I reflected thus: 'I am all the head now, and I shall soon be free.' I passed around the brain as if it were hollow, compressing it and its membranes slightly on all sides towards the centre, and peeped out between the sutures of the skull, emerging like the flattened edges of a bag of membranes! I recollect distinctly how I appeared to myself something like a jelly fish as regards colour and form! As I emerged, I saw two ladies sitting at my head. I measured the distance between the head of my cot and the knees of the lady opposite the head and concluded there was room for me to stand, but felt considerable embarrassment as I reflected that I was about to emerge naked before her, but comforted myself with the thought that in all probability she would not see me with her bodily eyes, as I was a spirit. As I emerged from the head I floated up laterally like a soap bubble attached to the bowl of a pipe, until I at last broke loose from the body and fell lightly to the floor, where I slowly rose and expanded to the full stature of a man. I seemed to be translucent, of a bluish cast and perfectly naked. With a painful sense of embarrassment, I fled toward the partially open door to escape the eyes of the two ladies whom I was facing, as well as others who I knew were about me, but upon reaching the door I found myself clothed, and satisfied upon that point, I turned and faced the company. As I turned, my left elbow came in contact with the arm of one of two gentlemen, who were standing in the door. To my surprise, his arm passed *through* mine without apparent resistance, the several parts closing again without pain, as air reunites. I looked quickly up at his face to see if he had noticed the contact, but he gave me no sign—only stood and gazed toward the couch I had just left. I directed my gaze in the direction of his, and saw my dead body. Suddenly I discovered that I was looking at the straight seam down the back of my coat. 'How is this, I thought, how do I see my back?' and I looked again, to reassure myself, down the back of my coat, or down the back of my legs to the very heels. I put my hand to my face and felt for my eyes. They were where they should be: I thought 'Am I like an owl that I can turn my head half way round' I tried the experiment and failed. No! Then it must be that, having been out of the body but a few moments, I have yet the power to use the eyes of the body, and I turned about and looked back in at the open door where I could see the head of my body in a line with me. I discovered then a small cord, like a spider's web, running from my shoulders back to my body and attaching to it at the base of the neck, in front. I was satisfied with the conclusion that by means of that cord, I was using the eyes of the body and, turning, walked down the street. A small densely black cloud appeared in front of me and advanced towards my face. I knew that I was to be stopped. I felt the power to move or to think leaving me. My hands fell powerless at my side, my shoulders and my head dropped forward and I knew no more. Without previous thought and without effort on my part, my eyes opened. I looked at my hands and then at the little white cot upon which I was lying, and, realising that I was in the body, in astonishment and disappointment, I exclaimed; 'What in the world has happened to me? Must I die again?..."

Now, if this case stood alone we should, perhaps, be right to explain it all as a dream. But it does not stand alone for there are numerous other cases to be found in the Proceedings of the S.P.R. and in Meyer's "Human Personality." In my opinion, therefore, it merits the most careful consideration and contains many points of the greatest interest and significance.

I think it will be found to work in remarkably well with the whole idea of the detachable quasi-physical replica, towards which hypothesis the whole of the observations in this chapter have been tending.

The narrator of the experience seems to think that the vehicle which he observed to become detached from the body and in which he was apparently functioning throughout the period in question, was actually the "Soul" itself, the permanent and immortal post-mortem embodiment of consciousness.

On the whole this seems to be the view taken by Mr. Carrington, who quotes the case, and to be that commonly held in France on the authority of MM. Leon Denis, Delanne and other writers. These latter refer to the organism in question as the "perisprit" and it is represented as being the vehicle by virtue of which the Consciousness persists after Death.

With this view I cannot agree.

I suggest rather, provisionally of course, that the Consciousness persists embodied in a four-dimensional vehicle to which the word "physical" as commonly understood cannot be applied at all. The replica, perisprit or "Etheric Double" as the Theosophists call it, is only the connecting link between the three and four-dimensional vehicles which, as we saw at the beginning of this chapter, must be supposed to exist if the four-dimensional hypothesis is to hold good at all. It seems likely that it is no more permanent than the physical body, and that it disintegrates after death in the same way that the bodily tissues do.

It is interesting to compare and contrast this case with the somewhat similar one of which a brief resumé was given on page 58. In each case the consciousness of the narrator was separated from the physical body but the conditions after separation seem to have been notably different.

In the first case the patient seems to have been independent of space in that he was able to pay a visit to a friend at a distance of about a thousand miles and to return in the space of a few minutes; while in the second he seems to have been tethered to his physical body by the "cord" to which he refers.

This is perhaps the most important point, but others are easy to find— notably in the apparent constitution of the temporary vehicle of consciousness.

It seems probable that in the first case the vehicle was four-dimensional while in the second it was the "quasi-physical replica" which we have been discussing.

It is with this supposition in mind that I shall examine the second case.

First then we notice that the narrator seems to have been in error in referring to what he saw interwoven, tissue for tissue, with the physical body, as the Ego. But this error was clearly a very natural one.

Although the point is not brought out with precision, the record seems to suggest that the narrator was viewing things with that internal or four-dimensional vision which I discussed in my remarks on Clairvoyance in Chapter III.

The process which is described as the separation of soul and body, I should prefer to describe as the exteriorisation of the "Etheric Double."[6]

As it happens, this exteriorisation does result in the separation of the Consciousness from the body, but to say that it *is* the separation would be liable to confuse the Consciousness and the four-dimensional vehicle with the Etheric double.

That exteriorisation should begin at the feet is only what one would expect from the known fact that the extremities are the first parts of the body to grow cold at the approach of death.

Throughout the account we notice the extreme plasticity of the vehicle in which the narrator functioned. It seems to have squeezed out of the body in a formless condition and then to have recovered its normal shape as soon as the deforming stresses were removed.

This is entirely in accord with the properties we must postulate for a substance which can, apparently, be moved and shaped by mere volition or at least by "mental forces," whatever that may mean, set in motion by the will. At first, that is to say during the process of extrusion, the Etheric Double seems to have been under the influence of some repulsive force acting between it and the body. This is admirably suggested by the analogy of the soap bubble.

When extrusion was complete, however, the E.D. "fell lightly to the floor." It was therefore composed of more or less ponderable matter, which is what we would expect from MacDougal's experiments.

The translucency and bluish colour are entirely consonant with the observations of Kilner on the aura, which, as already mentioned, I believe to be closely associated with the E.D.

The part about the clothes is curious and I am not prepared to hazard any explanation about it, beyond a very tentative proposal of auto-suggested hallucination.

Scarcely less odd is the apparent ability to use both the physical eyes and those belonging to the E.D.

But the fact that the latter were in operation is concordant with the observation of Durville that the sense organs of the exteriorised E.D. were operative in his experiments.

The small cord connecting the E.D. with the physical body is also in accordance with his observations.

On the whole then I think it fair to claim that this case fits in admirably with the experimental work I have quoted.

There is one other source of information which may profitably be considered here, namely the statements of the clairvoyants and of the Occultists.

I hope that the criticisms which I have been moved to make about the Occultists in preceding passages have been sufficiently stringent to clear me of any suspicion of being unduly credulous or over-ready to accept their statements as authoritative.

There are many things in their methods and their teachings which excite my distrust and antipathy.

None the less I think it foolish to ignore every statement which happens to be supported by, or to form part of, Occult doctrine.

I think it highly probable for instance that clairvoyant descriptions of facts concerning the Etheric Double are often reliable.

We have seen that the whole question of its study is probably a matter of observing, directly or indirectly, by ultra-violet light. We also have reason to suppose that the retina of the eye can be rendered abnormally sensitive to light of this frequency by artificial means.

But if such abnormal retinal sensibility can be induced artificially, it is very probable that it may sometimes occur naturally.

Hence, if the E.D. actually exists, as the evidence undeniably suggests, it is not only possible but probable that certain people will be able to see it without invoking artificial aid.

It must be remembered that observations of this kind contain, in themselves, no sort of "supernatural" element, although they may, of course, receive the most strange and erroneous interpretations at the hands of the uninformed.

When we turn to Occult literature we find that the theory of the E.D. is worked out in considerable detail. It is said to be violet-grey or blue-grey in colour and to interpenetrate the physical body. The "health aura," *i.e.*, the physical aura dealt with by Dr. Kilner, is said to be that part of the E.D. which projects beyond the physical body.

It is stated that the physical body and the E.D. are not normally separated during life, although in certain nervous conditions the E.D. may be more or less extruded from the physical body. (Compare this with the diagnostic researches of Kilner.)

"Anæsthetics drive out the greater part of the E.D., so that consciousness cannot either affect or be affected by the dense (physical) body. In the abnormally organised persons called mediums, dislocation of the etheric and dense bodies easily occurs, and the E.D., when extruded, largely supplies the physical basis for 'materialisations' (and for Crawford's structure. W.W.S.)."

"In sleep, when the consciousness leaves the physical vehicle which it uses during waking life, the dense and etheric bodies remain together.... At what is called death the etheric double is drawn away from its dense counterpart by the escaping consciousness; the magnetic tie existing between them during earth life is snapped asunder...."

(Taken from "The Ancient Wisdom.")

In other passages it is stated that the E.D. is connected with the physical body by a filamentary structure, "The silver cord," and that so long as this is unbroken it is possible for connection between Consciousness and the physical body to be re-established, but that when it is broken as occurs in death, the separation is final.

Finally it is definitely stated that this E.D. is a quasi-physical structure, disintegrates in the same way as the physical body and is perceived by a mere heightening of the ordinary visual faculty.

Let it be clearly understood that I do not wish one whit more importance to be attached to this last-quoted evidence than each individual reader may choose to assign to it and I fully sympathise with those who prefer to allow it no weight at all.

I have myself a strong penchant in favour of good hard scientific experiments with apparatus and, if the clairvoyant testimony stood by itself without any experimental evidence to support it, I should make no mention of it here. But I think that in common justice we ought to admit that the statements of the clairvoyants are, in the main, in close agreement with what we should expect from the indications afforded us by the experimental work which has at present been done. In continuing the latter we shall be well advised to keep the former in our minds as furnishing, at least, useful hints for our guidance.

On the strength of the various considerations discussed above, I am disposed to extend the four dimensional hypothesis as follows:

"Connection between the three- and four-dimensional vehicles is maintained by means of a substance of peculiar properties, which is intimately connected with the nervous system in the conscious functioning of which it is an essential factor. States of partial or total anæsthesia or insensibility are accompanied and probably caused by the extrusion of this substance from the body."

We are now faced by the problem of the constitution of this substance.

To this there would appear to be two possible solutions.

The first of these is that favoured, apparently, by the occultists and the exponents of the "perisprit" doctrine. The second is that to which I am personally inclined at present.

According to the former of these two hypotheses, the E.D. is composed of a sort of "rarified matter" by which, I take it, is meant matter possessing a smaller complexity of organisation than that with which we are normally acquainted. This would appear to be more especially the Occult view; although on technical details of this kind there is a somewhat unfortunate lack of precision and even of unanimity among Occult authorities.

A variation on this is the idea that whereas ordinary matter is the result of vibratory, or other periodic, disturbances in the ether of a certain frequency, the "matter" of which the E.D. is composed is the result of similar disturbances of a greater frequency; that it is matter transposed into a higher key so to speak.

The experiments of Le Bon, who claims to have obtained a temporary condition of equilibrium in the dissociation products of matter, are sometimes adduced as supporting this hypothesis.

For my part I have grave doubts as to the correctness of this view.

In the first place, there is nothing in Le Bon's work to indicate that these dissociation products are capable of being brought into a state of such very stable equilibrium as must be possessed by the constituents of the E.D.

In the second, the hypothesis involves us in all the difficulties which render so unsatisfactory all attempts to account for post-mortem existence on normal physical lines.

For, on either hypothesis, the E.D. is either the post-mortem vehicle itself, as held by the French savants, or it is the connecting link between the two vehicles, as I consider.

If the latter is the case, then in all probability the post-mortem vehicle is to the E.D. as the E.D. is to the physical body. If the E.D. is merely rarified matter then the post-mortem vehicle is probably merely doubly-rarified matter.

For this and other reasons I prefer the idea that the E.D. is composed of matter having an abnormal four-dimensional complexity.

Indeed, as I pointed out at the beginning of this chapter, this view seems to be a necessary corollary of the whole four-dimensional hypothesis I have been advocating.

It is very possible that we shall be compelled to reject the hypothesis *in toto* in the light of future research, but until this becomes necessary I think that my present view of the nature of the E.D. is the only tenable one.

Whether this abnormal four-dimensional complexity is molecular or atomic in its nature, or whether it is neither, I am not prepared to say.

The points in this chapter which I would wish to emphasise are, first, that if the four-dimensional hypothesis be true, there should exist a connection between the three- and four-dimensional vehicles.

Secondly, that this link should possess properties of a peculiar nature distinguishing it from ordinary physical substances.

Thirdly, that there are distinct evidences to be found in very independent quarters which strongly indicate that such a connecting link or substance does in fact exist.

Fourthly, that this substance does present unusual features, as for instance, susceptibility to volitional control and to forces which appear to be applied from some direction unknown to us (vide my remarks on the theory of Crawford's structure in Chapter III).

Finally, that, as it appears to be intermediate between the physical body and the post-mortem vehicle, it is well worthy of the closest study.

It will be very evident to my readers that this chapter is "extrapolatory" and speculative in the highest degree. The ideas discussed are based on experiments which are very far from being conclusive. I should be sorry indeed to guarantee them all as being of cast-iron reliability and I have no doubt that comparatively few will ever receive the amount of confirmation which is necessary before we can accept such things as proven facts.

Still, tenuous as the evidence is, it all seems to point in the same sort of direction and I have therefore thought it worth while to give it the benefit of the doubt and see what could be made of it on the temporary assumption that it is really reliable.

FOOTNOTES:

[5] Note the insensibility.—W.W.S.

[6] NOTE.—In future I shall borrow the term "Etheric Double" from the Theosophists and use it instead of the rather cumbrous phrase "Quasi-physical replica." I do not think that the term Etheric Double is a good one, but it is in common use, and I will adopt it until some better word is suggested.

CHAPTER VIII

THE RELIGIOUS ASPECTS OF THE HYPOTHESIS

Although I have no wish to become involved in controversial theology, I feel it incumbent on me to examine briefly the question of whether a general acceptance of the four-dimensional hypothesis would be fraught with any considerable consequences in the sphere of religious thought.

No one venturing to advocate conceptions so far-reaching as those I have been discussing, would be justified in ignoring their relation to any important stream of thought with which they might be held liable to come in contact. And it is evident that any hypothesis formulated, however tentatively, as a solution to the problems of Survival of Death and the nature of post-mortem conditions, must inevitably come into very close contact with Religion.

I shall try to show that it is a matter of contact only and not of conflict.

Even so, I might have omitted the present discussion had I not found a tendency, on the part of certain representatives of orthodox theology, to deprecate any attempt to find an intelligible solution to the problems involved.

It must be clearly understood that I am not concerned here with the defence of Psychical Research as a means of investigation, but only with the legitimacy of the end.

Generally speaking, those with whom I am so unfortunate as to disagree on this matter accuse me on two counts.

First it is suggested that I am attempting to advance by Reason or Sight rather than by Faith and, secondly, I am told that to "explain" such a matter as the Survival of Death or the nature of the connection between matter and spirit, would tend to reduce everything to terms of mere mechanism and to leave no place at all in the Cosmos for Divine Will and Purpose or for the transcendental and mystical aspects of religion.

I need hardly say that I violently resent both these accusations.

The first charge seems to me to be easy of refutation.

In the first place the idea of "Blind Faith" or "Unreasoning Belief" is one which involves a contradiction in terms.

As Whately well says in his "Logic":

"If a man resolves that he will implicitly receive *e.g.*, in religious points, all the decisions of a certain Pastor, Church or Party, he has in doing so performed one act of private judgment (*i.e.*, the result of reasoning), which includes all the rest."

Hence it is impossible to dissociate Faith and Reason.

Secondly, just as Courage, in its proper sense, does not mean feeling no fear but the overcoming of it; so Faith consists, not of having no doubts but of dispelling them, and this involves a deliberate exercise of the will in choosing between two possible alternatives; that is to say, an act of reasoning.

Thirdly, I submit that Life is not a sort of crazy competition in which special awards are to be received for completing the course blindfold, but a phase in the general upward progress of man—whether considered collectively or individually—and that consequently any knowledge is desirable which will enable us consciously and intelligently to co-operate in the process.

Finally, and I think that this puts the whole matter in one sentence, however clearly a man can see, he must still be able to believe his eyes.

However plainly we can see the path, we must still believe that it leads in the right direction, however conclusively we may demonstrate a proposition, we are still dependent on our Faith in the validity of Reason and the veridicity of the observations on which it is based—and this is equally the case whether the latter be scientific measurements or spiritual experiences.

The supreme effort of Faith, made by the most material of scientists no less than by the Saint, is the belief that the Cosmos, of which Reason is a part, is a coherent whole and not a Chaos.

The second argument appears to me to be equally fissiparous.

In the first place I should never dream of attempting to reduce the whole Cosmos to terms of mechanism.

Any such idea would be infinitely repugnant to me. Moreover, the attempt would inevitably be foredoomed to failure since there are problems which are essentially insoluble. The first and most obvious of all—the problem of the nature and origin of Consciousness—is one to which we can never hope to find an answer.

But quite apart from all this I entirely fail to see why the explanation of mechanism, using the word in its widest sense, should have any bearing on religion at all.

Religion, by which I mean something more than a mere code of morals, is concerned rather with motives than with methods.

If a child were to ask one why the sun and moon did not fall on to the earth, one might reply to the effect that they were prevented from doing so by the exercise of the Divine Will. Alternatively one might embark on a disquisition about the law of gravitation and planetary mechanics.

The two forms of explanation would be by no means mutually exclusive since the second does no more than expand the first by an exposition of the means employed.

If, as required by the Christian religion, we believe in the survival of the individual personality after death, it is evident that this survival must take place by virtue of certain properties inherent in the Cosmos and the necessity of Faith in our ultimate destiny will not be affected by any determination of the nature of those properties.

If our Consciousness does in fact persist after death it must do so in some state of embodiment, since the idea of pure essence is inconceivable.

For my part I utterly fail to understand why the study of the nature of the vehicle in which the consciousness functions after death, or of the conditions in which it lives, has any more to do with religion, in the proper sense of the term, than the study of the physical body and the physical world.

I need hardly say that I do not anticipate that Psychic Research will confirm the idea of the old-fashioned conventional Heaven and Hell of harps and crowns on the one hand and fire and brimstone on the other. But it would be a bold person who would be prepared to maintain now-a-days that these ideas form an integral part of Christianity.

Modern research on Evolution and the process of natural selection have somewhat notably discounted the story of Adam and Eve in the garden of Eden, considered as historical fact. But it would be difficult to maintain that the Christian religion has suffered as a consequence.

The account of the creation given in Genesis has had to be re-interpreted in the light of geological and astronomical knowledge, but Christianity is as vital a force in the world to-day as it was when that account was taken literally word for word.

Even so, if any specific revelation existed on the subject of the manner of survival, if, for instance, any of the words of Christ could be held to contain any precise information on the subject, it might be contended that no further knowledge was necessary. But this is not the case.

Immortality is insisted on, but nothing specific is said of the conditions by virtue of which it obtains. Nor, so far as I am aware, is any veto laid on endeavours to ascertain those conditions.

I repeat that in my opinion, cosmic mechanism and religion are distinct, and no knowledge, however full, as to the former can possibly either impair or replace the latter.

In short I do not see that the necessity for religion as an integral part of life would be one whit diminished even supposing we knew as much about the "next world" and conditions of life therein, as we know of this.

And this contention holds good no matter what results research may bring to light, no matter how much they may differ from our preconceived ideas.

For the truth is there all the time although at the moment we may not have grasped it and the Christian religion, if it be the true religion, as we believe, was framed, so to speak, to meet the needs of a cosmos organised in this particular way and in no other.

Unless, therefore, the Christian religion be false, it is impossible that the results of research, supposing them to be accurate and reliable,—a matter which can only be ensured by the exercise of scientific reason,—should in any way conflict with religious truth.

In case any one should feel that I ought to specify more precisely than I have done, what I mean by the Christian religion, I would refer them to the Nicene creed. Or if it is a matter of the interpretation of this in terms of conduct, I should cite "My duty towards God" and "My duty towards my neighbour" in the Church Catechism. Or in secular writings I would mention that view of Christianity which is defended by Mr. G.K. Chesterton in his book "Orthodoxy."

With these I am prepared to stand four-square, although it is conceivable that I might find myself at variance with some authorities on the precise interpretation to be given to certain clauses, as for instance "the resurrection of the dead" in the first mentioned.

But controversies about interpretation have been rife among Christian theorists from the earliest times and differences of opinion on minor points do not constitute lack of adherence in fundamentals.

Hitherto in this discussion I have been concerned only with negatives. That is to say I have been trying to show that there is nothing in the attempt which has led me to adopt the four-dimensional hypothesis which is in any way contrary to the essential teachings of Christianity.

There is however a positive side to the question.

I believe that so far from being antagonistic to Christian teaching, the general acceptance of the hypothesis would be of real value, in that it would put into the hands of the Church a very powerful weapon for the repelling of a certain form of attack, that of the scientific materialist to wit.

I do not mean to claim this as a merit of the four-dimensional hypothesis as such, for it would equally accrue to any other hypothesis which might prove to be true.

In the second chapter I gave my reasons for believing that the establishing of some such hypothesis would be calculated to remove the principle cause of dissension between religious and materialistically scientific thinkers. I there pointed out that the chief strength of the materialist lay in the reluctance or inability of the Church to give an intelligible explanation of the terms used in speaking of certain religious and spiritual matters.

I have explained that I see nothing in anyway repugnant to religion in the attempt to formulate an hypothesis to explain the mechanism of survival, etc.

Equally it should be observed that religion, considered as something more than a mere ethical and moral code, would be in no way freed from the necessity of justifying itself, *qua* religion, by the acceptance, however unanimous, of this or any other hypothesis. Such justification is a matter for an apologetic of quite another order, of which order, by the way, I regard Mr. Chesterton's "Orthodoxy" mentioned above as a very admirable example.

What the general acceptance of such an hypothesis would do, would be finally and for ever to deprive the materialist of the possibility of maintaining that matter, as he knows it, is the final and only permanent reality and that Spirit therefore cannot exist.

It is true that this would only involve driving him back one stage. If we suppose for the sake of argument that we could finally attain to as complete a knowledge of the "next world" as we at present possess of this, he could always return to the attack, using with regard to that state the same arguments as he originally used with regard to this. But having once broken through the ring fence of matter and demonstrated that there exist other realities of which he was at one time entirely ignorant, he could never deny that there might still be realms as yet unknown to him. He could never catch us again, so to speak.

I admit that the above is a somewhat fantastical supposition and scarcely within the sphere of practical politics, but the point is, that until we are prepared to give an intelligible explanation of things we are pent up in a sort of intellectual *cul-de-sac* bounded by matter. We may know, as the result of personal experience, that there is a way out, that matter is not the only reality; but our knowledge is a purely personal affair and the scientist is perfectly entitled, if he wishes, to decline to take the steps that led to the experiences which have convinced us, to dismiss them as mere hallucinations and to write off our alleged "revelations" as superstitious myths.

But let us once demonstrate to him, in a manner calculated to appeal to his intellect, that there may be a non-material reality and the *cul-de-sac* is at once broken through and becomes a vista.

It may be one of which we cannot see the end, and we shall certainly require faith to believe that it leads to the right destination, but the point is that it *is* a vista and not a *cul-de-sac*.

This is where I am convinced that the adoption of some hypothesis of the same general order as that which I have been advocating would prove of definite value to the Church and that is why I am so strongly of opinion that the Church, by which term I mean more especially those whose business it is to concern themselves with the general trend of Christian policy with regard to contemporary thought, ought to encourage and not to deprecate or oppose attempts on these lines.

In thus venturing to criticise the Church, I should like to make it clear that I only do so because I am convinced that the Church is a vital and indispensable part of human life, and because I wish to see her influence increased and extended rather than diminished. If I thought otherwise I should not take the trouble even to criticise.

So far I have said nothing about the religious significance of the four-dimensional hypothesis as such; considered that is to say as to its four-dimensionality and not merely in its capacity as a hypothesis.

The reason for this omission is simply that I do not consider that there is any such significance.

In the main concept of existence in four-dimensional space after death there is, so far as I can see, nothing either to contradict or to confirm anything taught by the Church except the bare fact of survival which both affirm.

I have carefully omitted all reference to the descriptions of post-mortem existence which have been obtained from time to time through mediumistic sources. Any such discussion would be both lengthy and out of place as it would involve a detailed critical examination of both the authenticity and interpretation of the pronouncements.

The only point about the four-dimensional hypothesis as such which I think at all likely to be called in question from the religious point of view, is that involved in the suggestion that Consciousness persists after death, not in the form of "pure essence" but embodied in some form of vehicle.

But this is a matter which is fully included under the general arguments I adduced in favour of the legitimacy of investigating the "Cosmic mechanism" to the utmost and there seems to be no need for a separate re-discussion here.

It is interesting to note however that a large number of the early Christian thinkers adhered to the view that "the soul" had some sort of material or quasi-material vehicle. A number of quotations on the subject are given in M. Leon Denis' book "Christianity and Spiritualism."

CHAPTER IX

SUMMARY AND CONCLUSION

I will bring this work to a close by a brief recapitulation of its more salient points.

A dimension is defined as "an independent direction in space." A flat surface is two-dimensional and the space we know is three-dimensional. The direction of the fourth dimension must be at right angles to every direction which can be drawn in our space and four-dimensional space is such that through any point in it, four, and only four, lines can be drawn mutually at right angles.

From every point in our space a line can be drawn running off in the direction of four space.

Consequently every point in our space is absolutely accessible from the direction of the fourth dimension.

The best way of drawing conclusions as to the properties of four space is by means of the analogy of the two-dimensional world; since four space is to three space as the latter is to two space.

The fact that we cannot perceive four space, or picture its nature to ourselves, is no proof that it is non-existent.

I suggest as a working hypothesis that four space is a reality and that Man possesses at least one other vehicle of Consciousness—a four-dimensional one—besides his physical body. In this vehicle he is embodied after discarding the physical vehicle at death and also during temporary absences from the body during life.

This hypothesis is likely to prove of importance in two respects. First, it provides Psychic Research with a working hypothesis which may be essential to its development as a science. Secondly the adoption of some such hypothesis should go far to remove the principle cause of recent cleavage between Religious and Scientific thought.

The hypothesis is capable of throwing light on a number of "Psychic" phenomena which are otherwise very obscure. It affords us a means of conceiving a mode of existence which is real and yet imperceptible to our senses, thus surmounting one of the chief difficulties in the way of conceiving of post-mortem existence.

In the realm of Clairvoyance it enables us to form some idea of the nature of the faculty of internal vision. With regard to Clairvoyance in space, it also helps us to some slight extent, although this phenomenon presents special difficulties of its own.

Other varieties of "out of the body" experiences are much elucidated by its aid.

The phenomena with which it is most closely connected, however, are those known under the general title of "apparent penetration of matter by matter."

To these it affords by far the simplest and probably the only explanation and, if they are regarded as irrefutably established, it will be difficult to avoid the conclusion that four space is a reality.

The *locus classicus* of such phenomena is the Slade-Zöllner investigation, but this is worthless as evidence. The literature of the subject abounds with records of similar occurrences.

The hypothesis also seems to offer a possible means of explaining the paradoxical rigidity of the impalpable structure discovered by Crawford.

The hypothesis may also have a certain significance, even in the realm of pure Philosophy. It enables us to conceive of the simultaneous existence of a series of three space simultaneities and, consequently, is of interest in the consideration of Time and of the possibility of Prevision.

It also works in well with a certain view of the nature of Vitality.

As regards its relation to ordinary physical science, we find nothing to conflict with it, but, on the contrary that there are a certain number of indications that four space is, as I suggest, more than a mere mathematical concept. It is possible that it may some day come to be recognised as having some significance in the theory of the nature of electrons and of ether, while recent views on "Relativity" strongly indicate that Physicists will soon regard the four-dimensionality of the Universe as a common place.

If the four-dimensional hypothesis is correct there should exist some sort of connecting link between the physical body and the four-dimensional vehicle.

The function of this link would be to deflect sensory impressions out of three space into four space thus enabling them to reach the Consciousness resident in the latter. Such a link must therefore be, in some way, intermediate between ordinary matter and four-dimensional matter.

That is to say, it must possess some degree of four-dimensional complexity. This may reasonably be supposed to endow it with peculiar properties.

If such a connecting link be found to exist in practice, it would tend to confirm the hypothesis.

The experiments of de Rochas, of Joire, of MacDougal, of Baraduc, of Kilner, and of Crawford seem to indicate that such a connecting link does, in fact, exist.

This is confirmed by the testimony of clairvoyants, which, though not of a nature to be rated too highly or accepted lightly, should be allowed some weight.

The attempt to formulate an hypothesis of this nature is not repugnant to Religion. Nor is there anything in this particular hypothesis which can be held to conflict with Religious doctrines.

On the other hand, the acceptance of such an hypothesis would cut the ground from under the feet of those who seek to maintain that matter is the only reality and that therefore Spirit and the Spiritual life are mere illusions.

No writer can expect to bring all his readers to his way of thinking. Indeed it would be unfortunate if he were to do so, as the effect would be to eliminate that element of critical discussion which is so fruitful a source of progress.

Consequently, I do not anticipate that every reader will agree with me. All I venture to hope is that I may have made good my contention that the four-dimensional concepts, in spite of the scorn poured on them as a result of the Zöllner fiasco, are worthy of very careful consideration as a tentative working hypothesis by those who are seeking to clear up the many obscure problems presented by Psychical Research.

If this little book is thought worthy of criticism, I shall welcome it. Its purpose will have been amply served if it succeeds in arousing interest in what will prove, I believe, a very fruitful field of speculation and research.

APPENDIX.

To illustrate how the analogy of the relation between two and three-dimensional space enables us to determine some of the properties of four-dimensional figures:

(1)

"Any figure in a space of a given dimensionality generates a corresponding figure in the next higher space, by moving in a direction at right angles to any direction that can be drawn within itself.[7] Or, in general, space of any dimensionality generates, by such a movement, the next higher space."

Thus, the lowest sort of space is space of zero dimensions, *i.e.*, a mathematical point. If it moves a distance of one inch, it traces out a Line one inch long—that is to say a one space "figure." If this moves at right angles to itself for a distance of one inch, it traces out a two space figure, viz., a square of side one inch. If this again moves a distance of one inch in a direction at right angles to every direction that can be drawn within it, that is, in a direction perpendicular to itself, it traces out a cube of side one inch, *i.e.*, a three space figure or "solid."

We must, therefore, conclude, from analogy, that if the cube were itself to move, a distance of one inch, in a direction at right angles to every direction that can be drawn in our space—in the unknown direction, that is, of the fourth dimension—it would generate a "higher solid" of side one inch. The higher solid thus generated is called a "Tesseract" and its properties are quite well known.

(2)

"Every figure, in a space of a given dimensionality, contains an infinite number of the 'corresponding' figures—see (1)—in the next lower space."

Since a point is defined as having "position but no magnitude," it follows that it would require an infinite number of points to make up a line.

Similarly a line has length, but no breadth or thickness, and it would therefore require an infinite number of lines laid side by side to make up a surface.

Again a surface has, theoretically, no thickness, and it would therefore require an infinite number of surfaces superimposed on one another to make up a solid.

We must therefore conclude, by analogy, that it would require an infinite number of solids to make up a "higher solid."

In particular, a Tesseract must be supposed to contain an infinite number of cubes, and, in general, four space must be conceived of as containing an infinite number of three spaces.

(3)

"The Boundaries of a figure in a space of any dimensionality are themselves figures in the next lower space."

Thus a Line (one space) is bounded by Points (zero space).

A surface (two space) is bounded by Lines (one space).

A solid (three space) is bounded by Surfaces (two space).

We must conclude therefore that "higher solids" (four space) are bounded by Solids (three space).

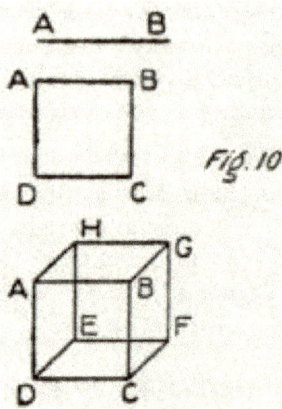

Fig. 10

To take the special case with which we are already familiar. The line AB, is bounded by the points A and B. (Fig. 10). The square, A B C D, is bounded by four lines AB, BC, CD, DA. The cube, A B C D E F G H, is bounded by six surfaces, namely, ABCD, CDEF, EFGH, GHAB, ADEH, BCFG.

Similarly we must conclude that a tesseract is bounded by cubes.

We shall see later that there are eight of them.

(4)

We may put (3) in a slightly different way, by saying that:

"Two adjacent portions of space, of any dimensionality, are separated by a space of the next lower dimensionality."

The portions AB and BC of the line AC are separated by the point B. (Fig. 11.) The portions ABEF and BCDE of the fig. ACDF are separated by the line EB. The portions ABEFGHIM and BCDEMIKL of the solid ACDFGHKL are separated by the surface BIME.

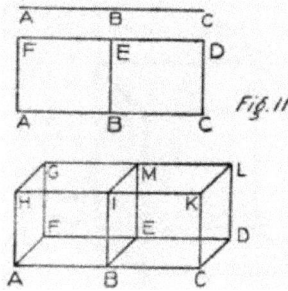

Fig. 11

Similarly we must suppose that any two adjacent portions of four space are separated by a three space figure.

Or, again, to alter it slightly, "any space is no more than a boundary between two adjacent portions of the next higher space." Whence it follows that the whole of our three space is but the boundary between two adjacent portions of four space.

(5)

"A tesseract, which is the four-dimensional analogue of the cube, is bounded by Eight cubes. It has Twenty-four plane square faces, Thirty-two linear edges, and Sixteen corner points."

This may at first sight seem difficult to grasp.

In reality however, it is quite simple.

We have only to remember that the tesseract is generated by the movement of a cube, in a direction at right angles to every direction that can be drawn in the cube, and that whenever a figure of a given dimensionality moves thus it generates a figure of the next higher dimensionality.

Thus every point in the cube will trace out a line, every line a surface, and every surface a solid, and, since the distance moved is equal to the length of the side of the cube, these surfaces will be squares and the solids will be cubes.

But let us first consider the analogous case of the generation of the cube by the movement of a square.

Let A B C D represent the original position of the square. It moves, a distance equal to one of its sides, in a direction at right angles to every direction that can be drawn within itself—at right angles, *i.e.*, to every one of its sides—and finally comes to rest in the position E F G H.

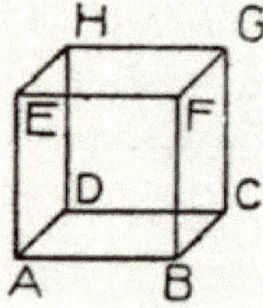

Fig. 12

Every side has traced out another square and we have, in addition, the old square ABCD, with which we started and the new square EFGH, with which we end.

Thus even if we had no idea how many sides, edges, and corners a cube had we could deduce them.

We should say:—

Every side of the original square has traced out a new square—that makes 4—and we also have the original square and the "final" square making a total of 6. A cube, therefore, must be bounded by 6 square surfaces.

Similarly we should reflect that the original square and the final square have each 4 linear edges, making 8, and that each of the 4 corner points of the original square would trace out a line, making new lines, and we would therefore conclude that a cube must have 8 + 4 = 12 edges.

Finally, since in a uniform motion no new points will be generated, we should expect the cube to have a total of 8 corner points, *i.e.*, the four corners of the original square and the four corners of the final square.

Now let us apply the same methods to the generation of the tesseract by the movement of a cube.

Observe that just as in the case of the square generating the cube we had the original square to start with and what I called the "final" square to end up with, so, in this case, we shall start and end up with a cube.

In the process of the movement every face of the cube will generate a new cube—that means 6 new cubes, since the cube must have had 6 faces—and there will also be the original cube and the final cube, making a total of 8 cubes all told. A tesseract must therefore be bounded by 8 cubes.

Similarly each line of the original cube will trace out a square. This, since a cube has 12 edges, gives us 12 new squares plus 6 from the original and 6 from the final cube, or a total of 24. A tesseract therefore has 24 plane square faces. Again each point of the original cube will trace out a line, making 8 new lines, and there will also be 12 lines in the original and 12 in the final cube, making a total of 32.

Finally, there will be 8 points in the original cube and 8 in the final cube, but none will have been produced on the way. So a tesseract will therefore have 16 corner points.

There is no reason why this process should not be continued indefinitely. For a tesseract may be supposed to move, in distance equal to the length of one of its edges, in a direction not contained in itself and will generate a *five* dimensional figure, bounded by ten tesseracts, and having in it 40 cubes, 80 squares, 80 lines, and 32 corner points. Thus a whole series of Higher Space figures may be produced. But these are of little practical interest, and I shall not deal with them here.

FOOTNOTES:

[7] NOTE.—The figures thus produced are not necessarily the strict analogues of the figures which generate them. For instance a circle, moving in a direction perpendicular to itself, would generate a cylinder; whereas the three-dimensional analogue of a circle is a sphere.

Booksophile
Your Local Online Bookstore

Buy Books Online from

www.Booksophile.com

Explore our collection of books written in various languages and uncommon topics from different parts of the world, including history, art and culture, poems, autobiography and bibliographies, cooking, action & adventure, world war, fiction, science, and law.

Add to your bookshelf or gift to another lover of books - first editions of some of the most celebrated books ever published. From classic literature to bestsellers, you will find many first editions that were presumed to be out-of-print.

Free shipping globally for orders worth US$ 100.00.

Use code "Shop_10" to avail additional 10% on first order.

Visit today
www.booksophile.com

www.ingramcontent.com/pod-product-compliance
Lightning Source LLC
Chambersburg PA
CBHW021508090426
42739CB00007B/516